SCEPTICISMS

To
MY WIFE

CONTENTS

CONTENTS

I

Apologia Pro Specie Sua

I

IT has not been my intention, in the pages
which compose this book, to deal compre-
hensively with contemporary poetry, nor
even, for that matter, to deal exhaustively with
that part of it which I have touched at all. That
sort of study has seldom attracted me. It has
been my aim rather to deal only with the most
interesting aspects of contemporary poetry, and
to do so in a manner which might provoke and
stimulate not only the casual reader but, odd as
it may seem, the unfortunate poet himself. Anybody must have been aware, as I point out repeatedly in the following pages, of the fact that the
present poetic era is one of uncertainty, of con-
fusion and conflict. New ground has been broken
in a good many directions, or ground which, if not
new, has been at any rate so long unused as to
have that appearance, at least, and to inspire a

SCEPTICISMS

certain amount of scepticism as to the resultant crops; and it has been engagingly natural, under these circumstances, that each poet should claim the most astounding properties for his own plot of soil, and become a little wilfully cynical as to the claims of his rivals. No one would expect much praise of Masefield or Abercrombie or Gibson at the hands of the Imagists, for example, nor, on the other side should one hope for much gratuitous enthusiasm over the Imagists or Others from, let us say, Frost or Masters. Those poets who, like myself, are critics of poetry as well, have had an almost unfair advantage in this situation. They have been able to articulate their particular theories, to argue for them in the public forum. It was a perception of the advantages of this sort of propaganda which drew the Imagists together under a somewhat specious symbol, and persuaded them to write prefaces in which the self-consciousness of the authors was just a trifle shrill, just a shade too "Noli me tangere"; it was a perception of the same thing that suggested to Alfred Kreymborg and others the uses of a periodical of their own, in which the nimble word-jugglers and sensation-balancers of that group—if it can be called a group—might juggle to their hearts' content, careless of ceiling or sky, and happily aware of a certain amount of audience; it was the same perception, finally, which has led Ezra Pound, Louis Untermeyer, John Gould Fletcher, Maxwell Bodenheim, Miss Harriet Monroe, Miss Amy Lowell, and myself,—among others,—to write, first and last, a good deal of criticism of poetry. We have all pretended pretty much, of course, in these cases, to write judicially. Our utterances are apt to sound authoritative and final. But do not be deceived! We are no surer of ourselves at bottom than anybody else is. We are, in fact, half the time, frightened to death.

II

Frightened to death, I mean, precisely of each other. . . . No one, I daresay, who is not himself in the game, would guess this. The usual opinion of us is that when we are not rolling our eyes toward heaven in fine frenzies we are rather a sanguinary lot, spoiling for fights in sheer love of bloodshed. When I am seen, for example, assailing Mr. Untermeyer, or Mr. Untermeyer is seen assailing Mr. Fletcher, or Miss Lowell is seen assailing me, the usual observation is simply to the

effect that "poets are certainly a vain and contentious lot of cockatoos." Well, vain enough we
are, in all conscience; but I do not think we are
by nature contentious. The fact is that we are
simply, as I said, afraid—mortally and secretly
afraid.

The reasons for this should be clear enough to
any one who will give his imagination to it for a
moment. What we are afraid of is the competition: a factor which few people are apt to consider
in connection with the success or failure of an artist, but one which is always in considerable degree
present, and which at the moment, as at all other
moments of artistic recrudescence, is extremely important. The competition among poets in this
country just now is, as a matter of fact, severe to
the point of deadliness. Not merely, I mean, in
the effort to secure publishers and publicity,
though few enough, truly, achieve even that
much; but more importantly in the next stage,
when, having secured a certain indispensable
amount of recognition, the poet begins to exert
himself in the most audacious and exhausting task
of his life, namely, to convince himself, his public,
and his fellow-poets that there is nothing accidental about his success, that his work has about it

a certain uniqueness of distinction which should commend it for perpetuity, and even that it may have, somewhat, the qualities of greatness. I do not wish to maintain that this undertaking is wholly conscious: but if the poet is not wholly or at all times conscious of it, neither is he wholly unconscious of it. And it is precisely of the ghastly possibility that his impression of himself may be wrong, that his undertaking, and indeed his life, —since the two are nearly synonymous,—may be only dust in the nostrils, that he is so secretly and so profoundly afraid.

In these circumstances, it is entirely natural that the poet, if he command a decent prose style, or is accustomed to the exactions of speech-making, should set about hunting converts. What he is going to say is largely predetermined. It will be, as it were, a slow distillation of his temperament through his reason. There will be moments of uncertainty at the outset, moments when his temperament goes too fast for him, and is not properly alembricated. At such moments his dicta will have a little too much, as he perceives later, the air of personal tastes and whims, and not sufficiently the carved serenity of, let us say, a poetic decalogue. But with time he achieves this stony solidity: his pronouncements increase in massiveness and weight. And many a young head is crushed beneath them.

III

It is not, however, the young heads which most attract his lithologues: it is rather the heads of an age with his own, and those a little older,—those that are bobbing, so to speak, for the same crown, —which most perturb him. This attitude is only human; though one would scarcely expect most poets to admit it with much candour. If our poet is, for example, an Imagist, who has been, let us say, pretty successful as a writer of short lyrics in free verse, conspicuous for their coruscations of colour, their glittering edges, and conspicuous also, in a sense, for their lack of conceptual or emotional elements, he will be a trifle sceptic about poetry which is narrative, or philosophic, or realistic. Let us perceive his case with care: let us sympathize with him profoundly. He is, let us say, hyperaesthetic, and exquisitely balanced; extraordinarily acute in his perceptions of sensory mood, miraculously adept in recalling, without allowing a single minute jewel-particle of colour to escape,

the most evanescently beautiful of the kaleidoscopic patterns of sensation which fall together,
and fall apart again, in the coolness of the mind.
This is his temperament, and, slightly dimmed,
this is his poetry. What must he conclude when
he encounters a Spoon River Anthology? He is,
of course, shaken to his foundations. He has
found, beside his dwarf Japanese garden, a foot-
print which looks colossal merely because it is
human. It signifies, for him, a world which is
only too bewilderingly huge, a world which in his
secluded course of refinement on refinement he had
altogether forgotten as perhaps containing the po-
tentials of poetry. His first reaction is an almost
stupefied realization of the minuteness and delicacy of his own work. His heart sinks: he sur-
veys this new thing with a mixture of admiration
and terror. "If the world likes this, what can it
find in me?" But habit and determination come
speedily enough to his rescue,— he needn't have
been afraid for himself. His vanity has been
growing too long and too sturdily to be so easily
overthrown. And his theory of art—which of
course is antithetical to that behind the Spoon
River Anthology — is complete.

SCEPTICISMS

IV

The stage, then, is nicely set for one of those little aesthetic altercations which give poets reputations as pugilists. Our poet writes an article on the Spoon River Anthology. Will it be an unbiassed article? Hardly. Too many things are at stake for him. The article will be honest enough: there will be no pretence about it, he will not conceal the fact that he admires the book tremendously, or that he thinks it contains certain of the qualities of greatness. But it will not be unbiassed. Directly or indirectly, from start to finish, no matter how far it may appear to be from the subject, it will be an impeachment of the artistic methods of Spoon River Anthology and a defence of the methods of the Imagist. The degree of intensity with which this will be done, and the degree of candour, will vary. Our poet is faced with alternatives. Perhaps his own convictions and course are slightly modified by the apparition. In this case he will admit the brilliance of it, but point out how much better it might have been had its qualities of vigour and incisiveness been more richly fused with the qualities of luminosity, delicacy, and precision. He has found a new ideal: a combination of divers new qualities with his own. This is a combination of which, as a matter of fact, he had always been capable; but, quite by accident, he has never till now perceived it. . . On the other hand, if our Imagist is a little more limited as to adaptability, if he feels that the qualities of Spoon River will always be somewhat alien to him as an artist (though he may appreciate them as a reader) two courses of action are open to him. The first will be to ignore Spoon River completely. It will be considered coarse and artless, its success temporary. He will be quite sincere in this opinion. Or, on the other hand, one can conceive him, just as sincerely, lifting his voice in praise of Spoon River, in the belief that the success of so different a type of work will hardly affect his own; and reserving his animosity for something a little more dangerously on his own ground.

v

It begins to be seen how complex is this life-and-death struggle among the poets. Our Imagist is only one imaginary case. When we recall that every poet is at bottom just as self-centred, just as determined to achieve and perpetuate a sort of pre-eminence for the poetic methods which his temperament, or sensibility, has forced upon him, we see into what a pandiabolorum we have strayed. We see also how much we must be prepared to discount anything that these amiable creatures start to tell us about art. Be they never so entertaining, be they never so grave and polite to their rivals, rest assured there will always be concealed somewhere a mortal sting. Some poets believe in employing the sting with candour and gusto,—some advocate that literary executions should be performed with an exquisiteness of tact, that the lethal weapon should not so often be bullet or bludgeon, or even a moonlit blade, but rather the serpent in a bed of roses, a poisoned perfume. One should not necessarily, I think, accuse the latter class of poets of being hypocritical. The method they choose is no indication of any timidity, they have no fear of violence, nor would it displease them to see their enemies go down under good red blows; no, if they choose the subtler and more Machiavellian method it will be because they believe it to be the more efficient, simply. "See," they seem to say, "how essentially good-natured, how candid and sweet we are! Could any one, under the circumstances, believe what we say of X to be anything but the most dispassionate aesthetic truth?"—Yes, this method has its advantages, as I have found. I used to be fond of the good old-fashioned sandbag. Miss Lowell once rebuked me for this: she warned me that I might become known as a "knocker." I thought she was wrong; but since then she has published "Tendencies in Modern American Poetry," and I see that she is right. The sandbag is too clumsy. And silence, as Ezra Pound can testify, is just as effective.

VI

The situation, then, reveals itself as one to curdle the blood. Who is to be trusted? Who will tell us what to like? Who will say "this is false, this is true, this is bad, this is good"? Who is there whom we can follow with soft-eyed confidence into the silences of the arcana? The answer, as should have been foreseen, is "No one." We are all unreliable, all grinding our own axes. About a good many things, things which do not too directly concern us, we can tell you the unvarnished truth. We may be pretty reliable on matters of aesthetic fact—most of us would probably tell you that too many sibilants in the same line are to be avoided, that vowel sounds can be combined so as to make a very pleasant harmony (an art which many poets neglect), that "The Man with a Hoe" contains a good idea but is a lifelessly written and mediocre poem. But the instant we go beyond simple universals, distrust us! You can be sure that consciously or unconsciously we are setting out to poison whatever springs we believe will flow down to posterity. We are determined to give those waters a tinge of our own. Every one of us is secretly afraid that unless we do this we are doomed to oblivion. Miss Lowell's "Tendencies in Modern American Poetry" says very little of "Men, Women, and Ghosts," or "Sword Blades and Poppy Seed," or "Can Grande's Castle": it is an opera in which the prima donna's voice is heard off-stage only and fleetingly. But it is none the less Miss Lowell who is the heroine of that book, and it is Miss Lowell's poetry which that book ingenuously and richly praises. Mr. Untermeyer's book, in the same way, is an oblique panegyric of Untermeyer: a quite deliciously naïve glorification of the temperament with which he finds himself endowed. How could it be otherwise? We are not really surprised at discovering this,—we should only be really surprised if we came across a case to the contrary, if we found Miss Lowell, in a fury of self-abasement, making an immolation of her own works before the altar of Ella Wheeler Wilcox, or Mr. Untermeyer forswearing poetry for ever after reading T. S. Eliot's "Sweeney Among the Nightingales." I exaggerate the point for the sake of emphasis. I do not mean to suggest that both Miss Lowell and Mr. Untermeyer do not very often, momentarily, escape the prisons of their temperaments and pay their respects to strains in contemporary poetry which they feel to be inimical to their own. What I do mean is that if you examine carefully the writings of any poet-critic you will find, a trace here and a trace there, the gradual emergence of a self-portrait; and one which is only too apt to be heroic size.

VII

This relativism dogs us even into the lair of the professional critic, the critic of poetry who is not himself a poet. In the magic pool of art what is it but the flattering image of himself that the critic parts the leaves to see? What indeed else *can* he see? We only perceive those things to which we are attuned; and no matter therefore how fine we spin a logic in defence of our tastes, all we do is subtilize the net of our temperament, the snare of our imperious desires, from which we are never destined to escape. We face here a disheartening determinism, we look across the abyss that lies between one individual and another, an abyss over which it seems almost impossible to communicate, and it begins to seem as if we should have to take refuge in that sort of aesthetic solipsism which, rightly or wrongly, we associate with Benedetto Croce and Professor Spingarn. If our tastes are mathematically determined by the sensibilities and temperaments with which we are born, and if any logic of aesthetics which we construct must therefore be mathematically determined by our tastes, of what use is any such logic of aesthetics? Of what use is it to talk of aesthetic values? Where all is relative, who will dare assume for himself the rôle of the absolute? Who has the courage to say, in these circumstances, "My taste is better than yours, and I have these reasons for it—"?

APOLOGIA

To the last question the answer is simple: we all have. Our self assurances are sublime. What is a trifle like aesthetic determinism? We know what we like, and we know that what we like is the best. What results from this, of course, is the feral competition among critics and poet critics which I have been discussing: it is the almost total absence of standard weights and measures which makes it possible. Success will be gauged, of course, by the size of the audience which we are able to attract and hold, the number of books we are able to sell. If art is a form of community expression, a kind of glorified communication (to quote Mr. Untermeyer) then it is clear enough, is it not, that at the present moment the best poets we have are Robert W. Service and Ella Wheeler Wilcox. But I hear already injured cries from other quarters. There are poets, I dare say, who will have the audacity to tell us that the figures should be reversed (such is the ingenuity of human pride) and that the poet who sells one hundred and nineteen copies of his book is really more successful than the poet who sells one hundred thousand. The audience, they will say, should be an intelligent audience,—not merely numerous,—and it should show a disposition to be cumulative, in increasing ratio, after fifty years.

And perhaps they are right. Perhaps, after all, this is the only sort of aesthetic decision we can come to; this gradual and massive decision of the slow generations, this magnificently leisurely process of accretion and refinement, particle by particle, century by century.

VIII

But this fact contains a ray of hope for us. Massive decisions like this are objective facts, and may well therefore be food for the behaviourist psychologist or the Freudian. If in the long run humanity prefers this or that sort of art, it should be possible to find the reasons for this, to say eventually just what chords of human vanity are thereby exquisitely and cajolingly played upon. Perhaps we shall be able to determine, in relation to great social masses, the law of aesthetic fatigue which precipitates those changes in taste which we call "literary movements" or "revolts." It may even become possible, at a given moment, to predict a new era of "realism" or "idealism." Or to predict, for that matter, if social changes go far enough, the legal proscription of certain forms of art—the romantic, for instance?—Or the death of art altogether.

IX

These speculations, however, are a little frightening, and I leave them to the psychologists, who, I do not doubt, will give those of us who are poets frights enough on this score before we die. For the present it will suffice to point out that since in the sphere of aesthetics all is relative,—or for each new generation, at any rate, relatively relative; and since this is particularly true just now, when experiment and innovation are so common in the arts, and give us so often work which cannot in any completeness be compared with works given to us by the past; it will be plain enough that a large part of the success of any such innovator or experimenter will depend on his own skill and persistence in making himself heard. This, at any rate, right or wrong, is his fixed idea. It is the fixed idea of pretty nearly every poet now writing in this country. We may pretend, sometimes, to be indifferent to our destinies, but at bottom it is a matter of considerable concern to us whether we can get our books published by Z.

rather than by Q., or whether, having been published, they are favourably reviewed by the New
York *Times*, *The New Republic*, *The Dial*, or
what not. Not that we value the opinions of
these journals—how perfectly idiotic they can be
we wisely perceive when, as not infrequently, they
presume to tell us what bad poets we are, or even,
in their incredible blindness, ignore us altogether.
But they command audiences, and we ourselves
wish to command audiences. If we are con-
demned to be among those gems of purest ray
serene which the dark unfathomed caves of ocean
bear, we shall know how to find, ingeniously, a
proud solace for that solitude; but we prefer—
do not be deceived by us for a moment—a well-
lighted shop-window on Maiden Lane. And we
make this preference sufficiently manifest, I think,
by the dignified haste with which we accept any
invitation to read or lecture, and the apparent
inexhaustibility with which we are able to review
books, particularly those of our rivals. It is a
cut-throat competition, a survival of the fittest.
We lose no opportunity to praise our own sort of
work, or to condemn that sort which we consider
dangerous.

APOLOGIA

X

The reader now perceives, I think, what he ought to expect of me. I am no exception to the rule. My own book is, in sum, just as clearly an ideograph of Aiken as "Tendencies in Modern American Poetry" is of Amy Lowell or "The New Era in American Poetry" is of Untermeyer. The papers that compose it were, almost all of them, reviews of books, and they stand pretty much as they were originally written. They represent my own particular attempt to urge the poetic currents of the day in a direction that might be favourable to me. I make no real apology for this: I merely maintain that I only do what all poets do. If pressed by some one seriously well-disposed towards me to admit some however tiny element of disinterestedness or altruism, I would probably,— like every other poet-critic,—confess that my sympathies are, perhaps, just a trifle broader and more generous than the average. . . . By which I would mean, subconsciously, that I merely carry my defence-reactions a little further afield.

I could, to be sure, have rewritten these papers in such a way as to have made a plausibly integrated unit of them—. I could have divided my book neatly into chapters on Realism, or Romanticism, or Vers Libre, or The Holophrastic Method; and I could have mentioned, for the sake of sales, every poet in the Cumulative Book Index. But to cover, as it were, all the ground, has never been my purpose as a reviewer, and I do not see why it should be now. My intention, in these papers, is to provoke and to stimulate: to single out for a certain careful casualness of illumination, among so many and such varied aspects, only those facets of the poetic tendencies of the day which are, for one reason or another, suggestive. In that sense the book will be found, perhaps, to compose a sort of unit, or comprise a gamut. That it contains no studies of such poets as Robert Frost or Edwin Arlington Robinson, poets whom I highly esteem, and whom I often have occasion to mention, is partly accidental, and partly because the works of both poets are conspicuous, in the contemporary medley, for precision and finish, and lack the tentativeness and uncertainty which provide for the critic his most seductive problems. For these omissions, and for the inconsistencies which indicate like milestones the tortuous course of my growth, and which the shrewd reader will discover for himself, I, therefore, make no apology.

APOLOGIA

The inconsistencies I could, indeed, have eradicated. They remain because it seems to me that in so relative a world they may have a kind of value. One is least sure of one's self, sometimes, when one is most positive.

II

The Mechanism of Poetic Inspiration

THERE is a widespread notion in the public mind that poetic inspiration has something mysterious and translunar about it, something which altogether escapes human analysis, which it would be almost sacrilege for analysis to touch. The Romans spoke of the poet's divine afflatus, the Elizabethans of his fine frenzy. And even in our own day critics, and poets themselves, are not lacking who take the affair quite as seriously. Our critics and poets are themselves largely responsible for this,—they are a sentimental lot, even when most discerning, and cannot help indulging, on the one hand, in a reverential attitude toward the art, and, on the other, in a reverential attitude toward themselves. Little of the scientific spirit which has begun to light the literary criticism of France, for example, has manifested itself in America. Our criticism is still a rather primitive parade of likes and dislikes: there is little inquiry into psychological causes.

Meanwhile, if the literary folk have been droning, the scientists have been busy. Most critics, at least, are familiar already with the theory of Sigmund Freud, that poetry, like the dream, is an outcome of suppression, a release of complexes. To the curious-minded this, however erratic or inadequate, was at any rate a step in the right direction. It started with the admirable predicate that after all poetry is a perfectly human product, and that therefore it must play a specific part in the human animal's functional needs. It at once opened to the psychologist (amateur as well as professional!), the entire field of literature, and in a new light: he was invited to behold here not merely certain works of art, but also a vast amount of documentary evidence, in the last analysis naïve, as to the functioning of the human mind,— in other words, so many confessions.

In the beginning, ludicrous mistakes and exaggerations were made. This was to be expected. Freud himself has steadily modified his position, as was bound to happen in the early and necessarily empirical stage of a new psychological method. There have been others, too, who have gone forward with the method, in a purely objective way, by trial and error. And the most interesting of them from the literary viewpoint is Nicolas Kostyleff, whose book, "Le Mecanisme Cérébrale de la Pensée," was published in Paris within a few years. In addition to much in this book which is of an interest purely psychological, there are also successive chapters dealing with poetic inspiration, the poetic methods of Victor Hugo, and the method of the novelist. M. Kostyleff does not pretend to have solved any of these questions. He is content with indicating a direction,—he does not attempt to delimit. He offers suggestions and observations that should be of tremendous value to the literary critic.

M. Kostyleff, in the chapter devoted to poetic inspiration, takes as his starting-point a belief that Freud's explanation of it as due entirely to hidden complexes, largely erotic, is insufficient. Certain types of poetry, notably those that approximate wish-thinking, clearly indicate such an origin. But what are we to do with the vast amount of poetry which cannot so conveniently be fitted into this category,—poetry, for example, which does not in any obvious sense appear to be the satisfaction of either erotic or merely aesthetic needs:

poetry, indeed, which would appear to belong to a cerebral rather than a merely emotional plane? M. Kostyleff here concludes, it appears wisely, that after all the writing of poetry is, like speech itself, a purely cerebral affair: and that it is not the result of a discharge of an excess of emotion in the poet so much as a cerebral reaction to external stimuli. This conclusion he at once connects with a theory, developed in earlier chapters, of verbomotor reactions: a theory that words, like other sensory impressions derived from contact with reality, are stored in the mind, not discretely, but in chains of association, where they become unconscious, and appear to be forgotten; but that upon a given stimulus these chains of associated words begin automatically unravelling, become again conscious.

With this theory of poetic inspiration in mind, M. Kostyleff approached various contemporary French poets and asked them to divulge the secret of their methods of composition. Among these poets were Madame de Noailles, M. Robert de Montesquiou, M. Haraucourt, M. Abel Bonnard, and M. Fernand Gregh. The explanations of these poets seemed at first sight to be rather divergent. Some wrote rapidly, some slowly.

SCEPTICISMS

Some conceived their poems in terms of visual line and space, some aurally in terms of music. Some started with the final or key line and wrote up to or around it, and some sketched rapidly in a sort of improvisation, later filling in and altering. But one fact began to emerge which seemed to be true of all: the fact that the initial impulse was almost always due to an external stimulus of some sort which effected, in a purely cerebral way, an automatic discharge of verbal associations, not necessarily attended by an excess of emotion. It became also apparent that the poets themselves were to a considerable extent aware of this. They sought to document themselves on subjects which appealed to them, so as to enrich their associations; and, further, they endeavoured to surround themselves with objects in some way related to the chosen theme, or to adopt, if possible, a suggestive environment.

This is already, it is clear, a sufficiently shrewd blow at the usual theory of poetic inspiration, that it is due to a tempest of emotion in the poet. But M. Kostyleff makes it even shrewder. On examining carefully the work of these various poets he found it to be almost invariably true that the emotional value of the completed poem far outweighed the emotional value of the original idea. The latter, in fact, frequently became quite insignificant. This would certainly indicate that the original impulse is merely a slight spring, which, once released, sets in motion a rather imposing engine. In fact, it was found in many cases that the original idea was either lost sight of entirely as the poem developed or actually contradicted. The explanation of this is simple, if the basic theory is correct. For if it is true that verbal reflexes function in associated chains, then we should expect the discharge of verbal reflexes to be self-generating, one set of associations to lead directly to another. No sooner does one flight of ideas come to an end than some overtone in it awakens further associations and another flight begins. And this was precisely what M. Kostyleff found to be true in his examination of many of these poems, particularly in the first drafts of them, with the many omissions, the many leaps to what at first glance might appear to be unrelated ideas. The completed poems, then, appeared to be not so much orderly developments of the original theme (which indeed in most instances could not alone offer the necessary amount of associations to account for the wealth or emotional power of the poem) as an accumulation of successive waves of verbo-motor discharge due to association, each rushing farther from the starting-point. In this manner we get a finished poem which far outruns, in emotional weight, the initial impulse. Of Mr. Bonnard's "Le Chant du Coq à L'Aurore," for example, M. Kostyleff remarks: "It is evident that this inspiration is due in part to a profound emotion before the beauties of nature, but the verbal discharge certainly surpasses it in extent, and can only be explained by the pleasure of renewing it. . . . And, everything considered, the emotion and the reaction to it are not equivalent. This explains also why in other cases the emotion can be slight, almost purely intellectual. In the preceding poem it is an emotion such as one feels, or can feel, after pleasure, which stimulates the imagination. . . . It is, before all, a play of cerebral reflexes . . . it is not an equivalent of emotion alone. It would never have become what it is if it had not had at its disposal great richnesses of memory, verbal and visual; which permit [the poet] to prolong the emotion, to renew it, and to communicate it to others." Again, of "Douleur" by Comtesse de Noailles, he says: "The feeling is always tender, but it awakens sometimes an exalted thought, sometimes a pessimistic thought. This proves once more that inspiration is not to be confused with the emotion which causes it. We saw it, in Bonnard, outstrip the emotional stimulus, we see it now in contradiction with itself; and that alone can explain the sustained flight of literary creation. If poetry were only an emotional discharge, it would be very much less complex than it is. In reality the emotional shock finds in the poet preformed cerebral mechanisms: mechanisms preformed by study, by meditation, by life. These are chains of reflexes which are not themselves kept in the brain, but the paths of which are traced there and easily reproduced. In a poet these reproductions are particularly easy, and the chains very numerous. The cerebral reflexes, becoming linked at the will of unforeseen connections, draw him along beyond the emotional stimulus. . . . Indeed, what matters the extent of the emotional power, since the principle does not lie there, but in the chains of cerebral reflexes, and since the latter can be set off by a stimulus wholly cerebral? . . . This obliges us to admit at last that poetic inspiration has two sources: the sensibility of the poet, and the preformed mechanisms of verbal reactions. These last we understand in the widest sense of the term, with the images to which they attach themselves, as also with quite precise qualities of rhythm and vocal harmony. A great poet is recognized not only because he is sensitive and vibrant, but also by the wholly personal qualities of this mechanism. And that is not a word of simple meaning. The personal qualities consist in the evocation of impressions which are not banal, and in the expression of them in a rhythm and sonority peculiar to themselves. . . . This formula seems to be important, especially for our time, when there are so many good poets—and so few great ones. . . . It is time to establish clearly in the eyes of the literary critic that to be a true poet it is not sufficient to have emotivity, internal fever, nor even a certain richness of cerebral images; it is also necessary to have a gift of verbo-motor discharge which is *personal*. For objective psychology, this presents something quite precise, the mental images being the cerebral reflexes directly associated with those of hearing and speech. This association is not innate: it is formed little by little from the first years of life. What is innate in the poet is a certain refinement of the sensorial organs. Seeing and hearing much as other children do, he must retain more memories, and better selected impressions. Each of these traces the path of a reflex; the visual and auditory reflexes are associated with definite verbal reactions; and at the time when his nervous system becomes rich enough to produce sensorial discharges, he finds himself already gifted with what we have just called the preformed mechanism of verbal reactions." In this connection M. Kostyleff points out that, as we should expect, poets are precocious as children, read omnivorously at an early age, and thus store up rich deposits of verbo-motor reactions, rich not only as regards sensorial impressions, but also as regards prosodic arrangement. And as evidence that the mature poet is not above enriching his vocabulary by conscious effort he goes rather exhaustively into a survey of the methods by which Victor Hugo was accustomed to document himself for literary creation, and into the rather elaborate system of auto-suggestion (through choice of environment, books, mode of life) by which M. Robert de Montesquiou induces in himself the proper frame of mind for work. And at the end of his chapter he concludes:

To be a great poet it is not at all necessary to have a temperament as pronounced as that of a Musset or a

SCEPTICISMS

Baudelaire. A delicate taste, if it be personal, may also serve as a basis for poetic inspiration. But it is the essential condition for this that the specific sensibility of the individual should determine for him the formation of an adequate mechanism of verbal reactions. . . . The number of parlour poets increases, and many of them lack neither emotion nor energy nor sonority of expression. In what do they fail of being true poets? The study we have just made directly answers this question. They lack a personal mechanism of verbal reactions. This mechanism is part of inspiration. It is formed long before the moment of discharge, from all that the poet reads or hears, and when the moment arrives, it begins to act without his being able to say whence the words come to him. Every one uses words, most words can be made into verses, but the more or less personal character of the latter distinguishes clearly those which are only an imitation, an echo of the poetic harmonies of the past, from the "sovereign verses" which leap from the mind of the poet as the product of a personal faculty for storing up and grouping verbal reactions. . . . Objective psychology finds here a very important contribution. To the factor revealed by Freud,—(the stimulus in the revival of psychic complexes,—) we see added another having an equally precise place in the organism, —an extraordinarily extended chain of verbal reactions.

M. Kostyleff does not presume, naturally, in reaching this conclusion, to have cleared up the entire problem,—he is probably as aware as any one that he has made only a beginning. For at once further baffling questions arise. To begin with, though we can subscribe without reluctance to the main tenet of M. Kostyleff's thesis that once set in motion a flight of poetic creations is to some extent self-renewing, ramifying by association from one group of reflexes to another; and though we cannot help being struck by the plausibility of his conclusion that the sole difference between the imitative and the original poet is in the more personal quality of the latter's mechanism of verbal reactions, it is clear that in this matter of the "personal quality" lies something which, though of very great importance from the literary viewpoint, is left rather vague. It will be recalled that M. Kostyleff makes a good deal of the fact that the poet, both instinctively in childhood and deliberately in maturity, seeks by reading to enlarge his vocabulary and the richness of his prosodic sense. But of course the imitative poet does this quite as much as the original one: if not more. His stores of verbo-motor reactions are acquired, presumably, in quite the same sort of way. Where, then, does the difference arise? In what manner does this store become, as M. Kostyleff says, more closely related in the one case than in the other to the poet's specific sensibility? It is at least questionable whether this distinction is not a false one. For, in a broad sense, no individual's store of verbo-motor reactions can be other than specifically personal to him. This would seem to force our search for a distinction backward one degree to the matter of sensibility itself. It would suggest a revision of M. Kostyleff's statement that imitative poets "lack a personal mechanism of verbal reactions" to a statement that, though fully equipped with such a mechanism, (many such poets have, even among literary folk, exceptional vocabularies) they lack any peculiarity of sensibility: they do not extend the field of our consciousness in any new direction. This would in turn indicate that M. Kostyleff puts undue emphasis on the merely linguistic aspect of the poet's function, with a faint, though perhaps unintentional, implication that language determines thought rather more than thought determines language. But may not a poet be great even if there be nothing remarkably original or bizarre about his work with respect to language or style,—great by reason of the poetic content, or thought, rather than for verbal or prosodic brilliance? . . . This brings us to the fact that there are two great tendencies in poetry,—two kinds of poetic value; and the classification seems to obtain for other arts as well. In one of them the emphasis is on the externals,—on form, style, colour, texture, with the intention of producing a sensorial effect as brilliant as possible; in the other the emphasis is on the content, and the style is made secondary, a transparent glass through which one may most perfectly see. Clearly, it is on poetry of the former rather than of the latter class that M. Kostyleff has based his conclusions: the lyric and decorative rather than the philosophical and narrative. For it is obvious at once that in poetry of the latter class the direction of the poem would not be dictated by the automatic unfolding of associated verbal chain reflexes, but, on the contrary, that the verbal mechanisms themselves would be directed throughout by the original poetic theme. . . .

If it is true, therefore, that M. Kostyleff has thrown an extremely interesting light on one mechanical aspect of literary creation, he clearly fails, indeed he does not attempt, to bring this aspect of it into relation with the aspect studied by Freud. We are shown parts of the machine, but not the machine in motion. What, after all, is the compelling power at the bottom of poetic creation?

SCEPTICISMS

If it were merely a matter of mechanical reactions, on a verbal plane, blind and accidental, it is obvious that one experience quite as much as another would cause a poetic precipitate in the poet's mind. But we know this not to be true. It is apparent that some selective principle is at work: some affective principle, or pleasure principle, which vitally concerns the poet. He reacts more acutely and more richly to some stimuli than to others; and even among these reactions he exercises a rigid system of suppression and selection. To be sure this power is self-generating, once started,—by accretion the affects intensify and perpetuate themselves, leaving always a richer deposit of associations, a greater capacity for prolonged cerebral response. But we must not forget that this selective principle has its beginning somewhere, that it is universal, that it arises in accordance with some need. Every man, as it has become commonplace to remark, is in some degree a poet. In consequence it is clear that in dealing with poetry we are dealing with something which plays some specific and organic part in the life of man. This, in default of any more plausible suggestion, brings us back to the theory of Freud. It is to some deep hunger, whether erotic or not, or to some analogous compulsion, that we must look for the source of the power that sets in motion the delicate mechanism, on another plane, which M. Kostyleff has begun to illuminate for us. It is clear that this is not merely a sexual hunger, nor an aesthetic hunger, nor an ethical hunger, though all may have their place in it. . . . Is it merely in general the hunger of the frustrate (which we all are) for richer experience?

However we answer that question, it is certain that such objective studies of literature as this of M. Kostyleff indicate for us a new method in literary criticism. With the clouds of myth and mystery blown away, we begin to see more clearly; we shall be better able to understand and to discriminate. And if we are thus made to see that literature plays a vital functional part in our lives, we must eventually begin to value our literature, *more consciously*, in the degree in which it fulfils that function.

III

Poetry in America

1917

LIKE the poor, Mr. Braithwaite's "Anthology" is always with us: a year passes, another myriad or so of magazines falls from the press, and once more Mr. Braithwaite has scoured them all, and gives us the result in two hundred odd pages. Examine, for instance, the Anthology for 1916. What new thing can be said of it? It does not change. It is six pages shorter than the year before; it selects for special praise only fifteen, instead of thirty-five, books of verse,—both of which abridgments are for the better. But whether through inability or unwillingness, Mr. Braithwaite seems no nearer learning that there can be little excuse for an anthology which does not select. Once more we have the clarion preface (a clarion uncertainly played) proclaiming that the present era of American poetry is to be compared with the Elizabethan and other great eras; a solemn catalogue of names held illustrious; and once more the verse itself follows on this with a harshly negative answer.

Is there any use in merely abusing Mr. Braithwaite for the many inaccuracies and hasty superficialities in his preface—for his cool assertion that Mr. Pound is the idol of those nimble acrobats who whirl and tumble through the pages of "Others"; that *Poetry* is Mr. Pound's organ of radicalism; that Mr. Kreymborg is the one poet produced by the "Others" group, or Miss Amy Lowell the one poet produced by the Imagist group; or that Masters, Frost, Oppenheim, Robinson, and Miss Branch dominate each a group-tendency? We have learned, I hope, to expect this sort of thing, and to discount it. We know that the affair is not so simple as this. We watch Mr. Braithwaite sliding over the smooth surface, and smile. But none the less, if we are to help poetry at all in this wilderness, we cannot rest content with amusement. Mr. Braithwaite is a standing warning to us that we must keep our wits about us; if every word that falls from Mr. Braithwaite's lips is a pearl of eulogy, we on our part must be prepared to utter toads of censure.

It is difficult to compare one of these anthologies

with another. The editor professes to see an improvement, to be sure, but if there is any, it is unimportant. What we can say clearly is that this volume, like its predecessors, is for the most part filled with the jog-trot of mediocrity. One must wade through pages and pages of mawkishness, dulness, artificiality, and utter emptiness to come upon the simple dignity of Mr. Fletcher's "Lincoln" (marred by a faintly perfumed close), or the subdued, colloquial tenderness of Mr. Frost's "Home-Stretch," or the sinister pattern of "The Hill-Wife," or Miss Lowell's delicately imagined "City of Falling Leaves." What else stands out? Here and there are pleasant lines, stanzas, poems,—but for the most part one gets an impression of amateurishness, of simply lines and lines and lines, all of them a little conscious of the fact that they are iambic, or dactylic, or anapaestic, or trochaic, or prose, all of them a little uneasy about their rhymes, their ideas, or the appalling necessity of somehow coming to an end. Here we have poets who, with quaint solemnity, tell us of " minstrelsy as rich as wine, as sweet as oil," who "parley" with stars, or confess to having "tears of awful wonder" run "adown" their cheeks, or describe the song of the swallows as their "spill," or proclaim themselves "cousin to the mud," or ask us to "list!", when they mean listen; and it is left to Mr. Untermeyer to reach the height of bathos in asking

> God, when the rosy world first learned to crawl
> About the floor of heaven, wert thou not proud?

What is one to say to all this—this inane falsifying and posturing, this infantile lack of humour or ordinary intelligence? How does it happen that it is only a scant dozen times in the course of these 184 pages that we find anything like a profound approach to the problems of our lives, or a serene and proportioned understanding of them, or a passionate rebellion at them, or anything, in fact, but clutters of thin sentiment, foolishly expressed, and dusty concatenations of petty irrelevancies? Is it Mr. Braithwaite's fault; or is it because we have nothing better to offer? Is there, then, any poetry being written in this country which we can hopefully put beside the recent work of the English poets—the work of Lascelles Abercrombie, Wilfrid Gibson, Walter de la Mare, or Masefield? I think we can make an affirmative answer; and in so doing, of course, we condemn at once the method employed by Mr. Braithwaite in the compilation of his yearly anthology.

For, as has already been said many times to Mr. Braithwaite, it is comparatively seldom that any of our magazines print poetry. Of verse, to be sure,—free or formal,—they print any amount: they are stifled with it. In some measure they have tried to respond to the wave of enthusiasm for poetry which has risen in America during the last few years, but they have proved pathetically inadequate. What, after all, could they do? Magazines can thrive only by reaching the greatest possible number. And the one essential rule for reaching the greatest possible number is to hold fast to tradition, whether ethical or literary, to avoid anything even remotely in the nature of subversion; or, if it becomes necessary through competition to advance, to advance with the utmost caution. The formal sonnet, sprinkled with "thou's" and "thee's" and exclamatory "O's," preferably calling upon the spirit of a nation, or addressed to a dead poet, or anything else dead, is the supreme gift. The exalted ode is a close second. And after these come the numberless hosts of the ephemeral sentimental,—all that we have been taught to consider good and true, brave and sweet.

It becomes apparent, therefore, that if we are to find poetry in America today we must look for it outside the magazines—in books. And this, of course, is where we do find it, such as it is. There can be no question that had Mr. Braithwaite composed his anthology from books, instead of from magazines, it could have been one thousand per cent better. It is not certain that Mr. Braithwaite could have done it, to be sure, for Mr. Braithwaite is not by endowment a critic: the evidence before us in this "Anthology" for 1916 is dumbly to the effect that Mr. Braithwaite is incredibly undiscriminating. What else can we say of the man who in his list of the fifteen best books of the year omits Fletcher's "Goblins and Pagodas," Masefield's "Good Friday," Masters's "The Great Valley," de la Mare's "The Listeners," William H. Davies's "Poems," the second "Imagist Anthology," Kreymborg's "Mushrooms," and Sandburg's "Chicago Poems," while he includes the very inferior "Songs and Satires" of Masters, "War and Laughter" by James Oppenheim, "Harvest Moon" by Josephine Preston Peabody, and other works by Bliss Carman, Adelaide Crapsey, Amelia

Burr, Charles Wharton Stork, and Rabindranath
Tagore? This is the plainest sort of critical
blindness. It is here not a question of being conservative or radical—it is a question of good taste.
A study of these juxtapositions will make it only
too clear.

If we are to take seriously, therefore, Mr.
Braithwaite's enthusiasms over contemporary
American poetry, as expressed in his preface, and
in his critical summaries at the end of his volume,
we begin to realize that he has damaged his case
at the outset by restricting himself to such verse as
gets into the magazines. It must be obvious to
any one that any such selection does our poets a
serious injustice: it is not, and in the nature of
things cannot be, fairly representative of our best.
The basic principle is wrong. For that we have
poets now who deserve to be taken seriously, even
if they are not Shakespeares, there certainly can
be far less question than there was even two years
ago. Since 1913 how much has happened! In
the autumn of 1914, Miss Lowell and Mr. Vachel
Lindsay first made themselves clearly heard. In
the spring of 1915, one after another, came the
first "Imagist Anthology," Masters's "Spoon
River," Frost's "North of Boston," Fletcher's "Ir-

radiations." And in 1916, a year in which for the first time in our literary history more volumes of poetry and drama were published than of any other class, we saw the publication of Fletcher's "Goblins and Pagodas," the second "Imagist Anthology," the "Others Anthology," Sandburg's "Chicago Poems," Kreymborg's "Mushrooms," Masters's "Songs and Satires" and "The Great Valley," Amy Lowell's "Men, Women, and Ghosts," Frost's "Mountain Interval," and Robinson's "Man Against the Sky." Of all these, Edwin Arlington Robinson is the only one who clearly reaches back into the period before 1914. Of the others, nearly all had been writing, and one or two had tentatively published; but in the main they are poets who have reached their maturity since 1913.

What are we to say of these poets and of their poetry? No one, of course, can say finally, "this is good and will endure"; or "this is bad and will perish." Any opinion must be personal, rooted in profound and for the most part unconscious predilections and prejudices, obscured by biases of friendship or the opposite, confused with questions of social, ethical, or philosophical character; and my own opinion, quite as much as Mr. Braithwaite's, is a ganglion of just such factors, and just as much to be guarded against and discounted. But having made this candid confession of our all-too-humanness, let us be candid in our opinions also.

To begin with, we must face squarely the unpleasant fact that, both in and out of the public press, we have been very seriously overestimating the work of contemporary poets: enthusiasm for poetry, and an intense and long-suppressed desire to see it flourish in America, have played the deuce with our judgments. In too many cases the wish has been father to the thought. Not only have we been undiscriminating, applauded the false as loudly as the true, but we have persisted in a sort of wilful blindness to the many and obvious faults of even our best. Bad leadership, of course, has conduced to this. We have had no critics whom we could trust. Miss Monroe and Mr. Braithwaite, to both of whom we all owe more than we can say, have, when all is said and done, been better drum-bangers than critics. Both have been somewhat insular in outlook, intolerant of all that is a little alien to them, intolerant of each other, and somewhat amusingly determined to find "great" American poets. Mr. Kilmer and Mr.

POETRY IN AMERICA

Untermeyer, both ubiquitous reviewers, the more elusive because so many of their reviews have been unsigned, have been equally limited, intellectually, and have left always the savour of cult or clique in their pronouncements. Two critics we have who stand clear of ax-grinding and nepotism, who analyse sharply, who delight to use words as poniards—Mr. Mencken of *The Smart Set* and Mr. Firkins of *The Nation;* but with these the misfortune is that they are essentially of the older order, and have an embarrassing tenderness for all that is sentimental, politely romantic, formal, ethically correct. The balance of power, therefore, has been with the praisers, with Miss Monroe, whose *Poetry* has manifested a tendency to become a sort of triumphal car for the poets of the West and Middle West, with Mr. Braithwaite, whose *Transcript* reviews have seemed at times to become a wholesale business in laurel wreaths, and with others, less fortunate in their power, of the same nature. And in consequence, even the most cautious of us have been in spite of ourselves somewhat infected by the prevailing idolatries. It has become habitual to accept, unpleasant to censure. When we criticize at all, we condemn utterly; when we praise, we sing panegyrics.

SCEPTICISMS

There has been no middle course of balanced and impartial analysis, no serene perspective,—above all, no taste. It seems as if we have not been long enough civilized, as if there were too much still undigested, or indigestible, in our environment.

We have therefore a group of myths among us, some or all of them conflicting, and sedulously encouraged by the publishers. A vague notion is abroad that Frost, Masters, Robinson, Lindsay, Fletcher, Miss Lowell, and others still who have not been quite so successful, are, if not great poets, at any rate brilliantly close to it. Whether this is true or not need not at once concern us. What becomes important for us, in the circumstances, is to realize that if these poets are as commanding as we think them to be, it is time for us to stop spattering them with unmixed praise—which we do under the quaint delusion that we are writing serious articles upon them—and look at them, for once, with more of the scientist's eye, and less of the lover's. We need to remind ourselves that they are flesh and blood, as liable to failures and mistakes as ourselves, constantly and sometimes desperately struggling for a precarious foothold, sometimes driven to foolishness by the keenness of the competition, sometimes exhausted by it.

What compels them to do what they do? What faults result from this, and what virtues? What can we expect of them? This is the sort of question we should be getting ready to ask them.

Turning upon them from this quarter, we should at once find them looking a little less imposing. We should begin to see first of all one great and glaring characteristic of practically all American poets: that, though rich in invention, they are poor in art. Exceptions to this there are, —notably, Edwin Arlington Robinson, who, perhaps, in other respects pays the penalty. But in the main that stigma touches them all. Most conspicuous in the work of Mr. Masters and Miss Lowell, it is by no means restricted to them alone, —few, if any, escape it. No clearer line of cleavage divides contemporary American poetry from contemporary English: we may prefer the greater richness and variety of the American, its greater relentlessness in search of realities; but the instant we turn to the English we feel a certain distinction, a certain intellectual and aesthetic ease and freedom, no matter on what plane—whether in the clear lyrics of de la Mare and Hodgson and Davies and Aldington, or the strange, powerful, almost laboured psychological episodes of Gibson, or the

intellectual spaciousness and tortuous energy of
Abercrombie. And this lack of distinction, this
inability of our poets to make their inventions
works of art,—to speak with that single-toned
authenticity which arises from perfect expression,
—constitutes the most serious menace against their
possible survival. Mr. Frost is our most consistent performer, of course,—we can place him
over against the English poets akin to him without
blushing. And Mr. Robinson, too, is in this respect dependable, though he tends to jingle, does
not command the power or the lyric beauty of the
others, and abuses his trick of veiled implications.
After this, we are in the dark. Miss Lowell,
Fletcher, Masters, have all done brilliant work
in their kinds,—but even the best of it is marred
by strange artistic blindnesses. They cannot be
counted upon. They write prose with one hand
and poetry with the other, and half the time know
not what they do. If one moment they select
carefully, the next moment they empty cartloads.
They seem for ever uncertain whether to sing or to
talk, and consequently try sometimes to do both
at once.

The plain fact is that we have been passing
through a period of ferment, a period of uncer-

tainty, experiment, transition. A great variety
of intellectual energies has been simultaneously
catalyzed by a great variety of stimuli, and the
result inevitably has been chaos. Realists have
sprung up, reverent as well as irreverent; romanticists have sprung up, radical as well as conventional; and in addition to these major groups have
risen detached individuals difficult to classify, and
other groups heterogeneously composed. Experiment is the order of the day. Desperation to say
the last word, to go farthest, to dissolve tradition
and principle in the most brilliant self-consciousness, has led to literary pranks and freaks without
number. Occasionally this has borne good results, more often it has merely startled. The
bizarre has frequently been mistaken for the
subtle; unselective treatment has been too often
considered realism. The Imagists, straying too
far in search of flowers of vividness and colour,
have ended by losing themselves in a Plutonian
darkness of unrelated sensory phenomena: they
predicate a world of sharply separate entities
without connective tissue of relationship, and, in
addition, have sacrificed a large part of their power
to convey this vision by their unwillingness or
inability to heighten their readers' receptiveness

through playing upon it rhythmically. Members of the "Others" group (if Mr. Kreymborg will permit it to be so called) have sometimes seemed determined to revert to the holophrastic method of self-expression which antedated the evolution of analytical self-expression and language. At its worst, the result has been captivating nonsense; at its best, it gives us the peculiarly individual semi-poems of Wallace Stevens and Maxwell Bodenheim.

This has been the background—of rapid change and experimentation, extravagance, over-decorativeness, variety, and fearless entrance into the penetralia of life—against which our major group of Frost, Masters, Fletcher, Amy Lowell, and Robinson have made themselves clear. They cannot be detached from that background. They are constantly modifying it, and being modified by it. A process of mutual protective colouration, of co-adaptation, is constantly going on. Where they fear, they imitate. In consequence we should expect to find the faults as well as the virtues of the background repeated in the protagonists,—and we do. With the exception of Mr. Frost (and even he has been slightly infected on the metrical side) and Mr. Robinson, our leading poets, one and all, seem to be writing with a constantly shifting set of values in mind: their eyes are on their audience and on their rival poets, but seldom if ever on eternal principles. The result is a kaleidoscopic effect of shifting viewpoints, and it has become typical of our most typical poets that their work seems to proceed not from one centre, but from many. Now it is lyric, now it is narrative, now dramatic, or philosophic, or psychological—and as the mood fluctuates so does the vehicle chosen, from the most formal through successively more loosely organized modes to the gnomic prose of "Spoon River" or "The Ghosts of an Old House." Our poets have not quite found themselves. They are casting about for something, they do not know what, and have not found it. And more than anything else it is this fact that gives their work that unfinished, hurried quality, impatient and restless, rapidly unselective, which makes it appear, beside English work, lacking in distinction. Like the spring torrent, it is still muddy.

It would be foolish to lament this fact. The Spring freshet has its compensations of power and fulness. It would be equally foolish to delude ourselves about it, to imagine that we are already in the middle of a Golden Age; up to the present point it is, rather, an age of brass,—of bombast and self-trumpetings. In the meantime, we can look to the future with considerable confidence that out of the present unprincipled chaos, rich in energies, we shall yet create a harmony. And we can take comfort in a relatively serene belief that Mr. Braithwaite's "Anthology of Magazine Verse" very seriously misrepresents—or, rather, hardly represents at all—the true state of poetry in America today.

IV

The Two Magics: Edgar Lee Masters

MR. MASTERS is a welcome, though perplexing, figure in contemporary American poetry. Welcome, because along with Mr. Frost, and perhaps Mr. Robinson and Mr. Sandburg, he is a realist, and because a vigorous strain of realism is so profoundly needed in our literature today—as indeed it has always been needed. Perplexing, because his relative importance, as posterity will see it, is so extraordinarily difficult to gauge. Of his welcome there can be no question. There has been a disposition among poets and critics of poetry during the last three years to assume that the most important changes, or revolutions, taking place in American poetry at present are those that regard form. The Imagists and other free verse writers have found their encomiasts, and to them the renewed vitality of American poetry has in consequence been a little too freely ascribed. No one will deny that the current changes in poetic form— the earlier blind revolt, the later effort to mint new forms which shall be organic—have their value. But we should not forget that of equal and possibly greater importance has been the attempt of our realists to alter not merely the form of poetry but also its content. What Mr. Masefield and Mr. Gibson did in England, it remained for Mr. Masters and Mr. Frost to do in America. The influence of "Spoon River Anthology" and "North of Boston" can hardly yet be estimated. That the Imagists did not share in this influence was perhaps merely an accident. There was nothing in the Imagist platform to prevent it. It simply happened that the Imagists were without exception lyric poets, or more specifically, poets in the decorative or colouristic tradition. While they were still experimenting with new rhythms as the vehicle of expression for a gamut of perceptions and sensations which differed from the traditional perceptions and sensations of poetry only by being a trifle subtler and more objective, Mr. Masters and Mr. Frost, without so much as a preliminary blast of the trumpet, suddenly incorporated into their poetry a new world—the world of the individual consciousness in its complex entirety. At the moment, this was a new conception of the nature of poetry. A poem was not to be a single jewel of colourful phrases, but the jewel in its matrix. Of such poetry, it is readily seen, the appeal would be not merely aesthetic, but intellectual and emotional also—in the richest sense, human. The distinction between the poetic and the non-poetic vocabulary was broken down, a condition which has obtained conspicuously only in two preceding poetic eras, the Chaucerian and Elizabethan. The opportunity for a transfusion of vitality from our tremendously increased prose vocabulary to the comparatively small and static poetic vocabulary was unparalleled. New developments of form were involved, perhaps, but while the immediate effects of these were more obvious, it is to be questioned whether they were as far-reaching. It is safe to say that no poet now writing in this country has escaped this influence. In its healthily acrid presence it has been increasingly difficult for the prettifiers, the airy treaders of preciosity, the disciples of sweetness and sentiment, to go their mincing ways. Most of them have felt a compulsion either to change tone or to be silent.

SCEPTICISMS

In view of the importance of this influence, therefore, it is interesting to speculate on the nature and function of realistic poetry; and the work of Mr. Masters furnishes an excellent opportunity. To say that such work as this delights us, at its best, because it is human, is after all somewhat superficial. In a broad sense, even the most treble of dawn-twitterers is human. But clearly the pleasure it affords us is a different sort of pleasure from that afforded, say, by a lyric of Becquer or Shelley. It has, when it is good, a clearly recognizable magic; but this magic is not quite of the same character as that we associate with "Kubla Khan" or "The Ode to a Grecian Urn." Matthew Arnold in his essay on poetry was apparently insensible to this distinction, for at least one of his famous touchstone lines belongs rather to the realistic than to the lyric category of magic. The line of Wordsworth, "And never lifted up a single stone," certainly does not appeal, in any clear way, to the sense of beauty; its felicity is of a different sort. What precisely constitutes this second sort of verbal magic is in the present state of psychology perhaps impossible to analyse. At most we can perceive certain relations and distinctions. On one plane, the mechanism of the two is identical: both depend for their effect on the choice of so sharply characteristic a single detail that a powerful motor reaction will ensue and complete the sensory pattern in its entirety. This is known as Pavlov's law. But here begins the divergence, for while this might explain the quality of *vividness* which is common to both, it appears to have no bearing on the fact that each sort of vividness affects the reader in a specifically different manner. The first, or Shelley-Becquer type of magic, appeals to what is indefinitely called the sense of beauty; the second, or Masters-Frost type, appeals perhaps to the sense of reality. These terms are deplorably vague. Our enjoyment of art is consequent upon the satisfaction of two kinds of hunger: hunger for beauty and hunger for knowledge. Let what the Freudians call an emotional complex be formed early in life upon the frustrated first of these hungers, and we get a lyric or colourist type of artist; upon the other, and we get a realist.

Mr. Masters is of the latter type, though there are traces in him of the former as well. The curious thing is that while he frequently manifests a vivid desire to employ the lyric kind of magic, he nearly always fails at it; his average of success with the realistic magic is consistently very much higher. He is essentially a digger-out of facts, particularly of those facts which regard the mechanism of human character. In the presence of richly human material—the sufferings, the despairs, the foolish illusions, the amazing overweenings of the individual man or woman—he has the cold hunger of the microscope. Curiosity is his compelling motive, not the desire for beauty. He is insatiable for facts and events, for the secrets of human behaviour. Consequently it is as a narrator that he does his best work. He is essentially a psychological story-teller, one who has chosen for his medium not prose but verse, a tumbling and jostling and overcrowded sort of verse, which, to be sure, frequently becomes prose. Was Mr. Masters wise in making this choice? He is by nature extremely loquacious and discursive—it appears to be painful for him to cut down to mere essentials—and prose would seem to be a more natural medium for such a mind. But while he almost always fails to compress his material to the point where it becomes singly powerful, it is only the fact that he uses a verse form which compels him to compress at all; and it is also clear that at his moments of keenest pleasure in dissective narration he can only experience satisfaction in a verse of sharply accentuated ictus. It is at these moments that his work takes on the quality of realistic magic, the magic of vivid action, dramatic truthfulness, muscular reality. We are made to feel powerfully the thrust and fecundity of human life, particularly its animalism; we are also made to feel its struggle to be, or to believe itself, something more. It is in the perception and expression of this something more that Mr. Masters chiefly fails, not because he is not aware of it (he repeatedly makes it clear that he is, though not of course in the guise of sentimentality) but because at this point his power and felicity of expression abandon him. What emotional compulsion he has towards self-expression lies in the other direction. His temperament might be compared not inexactly to that of Hogarth, the Hogarth of "Marriage à la Mode" and "The Rake's Progress" rather than of the caricatures. It is in the Hogarthian type of magic that he is most proficient.

Is it certain however that this proficiency is sufficient to make his work enduring? There is no other poet in America today whose work is so amazingly uneven, whose sense of values is so

disconcertingly uncertain. While in some respects Mr. Master's intellectual equipment is
richer than that of any of his rivals, it has about
it also something of the *nouveau riche*. Much
of his erudition seems only half digested, much
of it is inaccurate, much of it smells of quackery
or the woman's page of the morning paper.
Much of it too is dragged in by the heels and is
very dull reading. Moreover, this uncertainty—
one might almost say unripeness—besets Mr.
Masters on the aesthetic plane quite as clearly as
on the intellectual. To put it synaesthetically,
he appears not to know a yellow word from a
purple one. He goes from a passage of great
power to a passage of bathos, from the vividly
true to the blatantly false, from the incisive to
the dull, without the least awareness. In "Songs
and Satires" one passes, in bewilderment, from
"Arabel," remarkably sustained in atmosphere,
vivid in its portraiture, skilful in its use of
suspense, to the ludicrous ineffectuality of the
Launcelot poem, in which many solemn events
are unintentionally comic. In "Toward the
Gulf," one passes, with the same astonishment,
from the utter falseness and preposterous anti-
climax of the "Dialogue at Perko's" to the in-

tensity and magic of "The Widow LaRue." This means of course that Mr. Masters is not in the thorough sense an artist. He does not know the effect of what he is doing. He is indeed, as an artist, careless to the point of recklessness. It is as if a steam dredge should become pearl diver: he occasionally finds an oyster, sometimes a pearl; but he drags up also an amazing amount of mud. His felicities and monstrosities are alike the accidents of temperament, not the designs of art. Hasty composition is repeatedly manifest. Six months more of reflection would perhaps have eliminated such poems as "The Canticle of the Race" (Mr. Masters is often in the hands of demons when he uses rhyme), "The Awakening," "In the Garden at the Dawn Hour," "Dear Old Dick," "Toward the Gulf," and two or three others; a good half of "Songs and Satires"; perhaps a third of "Spoon River"; and would have disclosed to him such verbal errors as "disregardless" and "forgerer"—trifles, indeed, but symptomatic.

And yet on the whole one is more optimistic as to the future of Mr. Masters after reading his latest book than at any time since the appearance of "Spoon River Anthology." Bad and good are still confounded, but in more encouraging proportions. From "Widow LaRue," "Front the Ages with a Smile," "Tomorrow is my Birthday," "Saint Deseret" one gets an almost unmixed pleasure. In these one feels the magic of reality. These poems, like "Arabel" and "In the Cage," are synthesized; and it is in this vein that one would like to see Mr. Masters continue, avoiding the pitfalls of the historical, the philosophical, the pseudo-scientific. Will he yet learn to employ, as an artist, the selection and compression which in the "Spoon River Anthology" were forced upon him by the exigencies of the case? Will he continue at the same time to develop in psychological richness and in his sense of the music of sound and the balance of form? . . . Whether he does or not, we already have reason to be profoundly grateful to him. His influence has been widespread and wholesome. We are badly in need of poets who are unafraid to call a spade a damned shovel. And a good many of us are too ready to forget that realistic magic is quite as legitimate in poetry as lyric magic, and quite as clearly in the English tradition. If art is the effort of man to understand himself by means of self-expression, then surely it should not be all

ghosts and cobwebs and soul-stuff. . . . Mr.
Masters reminds us that we are both complex and
physical.

V

The Function of Rhythm: Ford Madox Hueffer

IN the preface to his latest book of poems, "On Heaven," Mr. Ford Madox Hueffer remarks:

The greater part of the book is, I notice on putting it together, in either vers libre or rhymed vers libre. I am not going to apologize for this or to defend vers libre as such. It is because I simply can't help it. Vers libre is the only medium in which I can convey any more intimate moods. Vers libre is a very jolly medium in which to write and to read, if it be read conversationally and quietly. And anyhow, symmetrical or rhymed verse is for me a cramped and difficult medium—or an easy and uninteresting one.

One recollects further, that Mr. Hueffer has in the past been also insistent, in theory and in practice, on the point that poetry should be at least as well written as prose—that, in other words, it

must be good prose before it can be good poetry.
Taken together, these ideas singularly echo a preface written one hundred and twenty odd years
ago—Wordsworth's preface to the "Lyrical Ballads." In the appendix to that volume Wordsworth, it will be recalled, remarked that in works
of imagination the ideas, in proportion as they are
valuable, whether in prose or verse, "require and
exact one and the same language." And throughout he insisted on doing away with all merely
decorative language and on using the speech of
daily life.

On the matter of metre or rhythm, however, the
two poets are not so entirely in agreement as they
might appear to be. They are in agreement, it
might be said, just in so far as they both seem
inclined to regard the question of rhythm as only
of minor or incidental importance. "Metre," said
Wordsworth, "is only adventitious to composition." Mr. Hueffer, as is seen above, candidly
admits that he avoids the strictest symmetrical
forms because to use them well is too difficult.
Do both poets perhaps underestimate the value of
rhythm? In the light of the widespread vogue of
free verse at present, it is a question interesting to
speculate upon. And Mr. Hueffer's poems,

which are excellent, afford us a pleasant opportunity.

Wordsworth's theory as to the function of rhythm was peculiar. He believed that as poetry consists usually in a finer distillation of the emotions than is found in prose, some check must be used lest the excitation arising therefrom, whether pleasurable or painful, exceed desired bounds. Rhythm is to act as a narcotic. "The co-expression of something regular, something to which the mind has been accustomed . . . in a less excited state cannot but have great efficacy in tempering . . . the passion by an admixture of ordinary feeling. . . ." Only by way of incidental emendation did Wordsworth suggest that in some cases metre might "contribute to impart passion to the words." This is perhaps to put the cart before the horse. Mr. Hueffer, on the other hand, while equally regarding, or appearing to regard, metre as a subsidiary element, raises a different and subtler objection to it. In common with a good many champions of free verse he feels that free verse is better than symmetrical verse for the conveyance of more intimate moods. This is a plausible and intriguing theory. At first glimpse it seems only natural that in a freer and more dis-

cursive medium the poet should find himself better
able to fix upon the more impalpable nuances of
feeling.   But a steadier inspection leaves one not
quite so sure.   If one can convey subtler moods in
free verse than in symmetrical verse, might one
not logically argue that prose could be subtler still
than either?   And we should have reached the
conclusion that poetry should employ, to reach its
maximum efficiency, not only the language but
also the rhythms of prose—in other words, that it
should *be* prose.

The logic is perhaps not impeccable; but it is
sufficiently strong to suggest the presence of some
error.   If prose could convey subtler emotional
moods and impressions than poetry, why write
poetry?   We suspect however that the reverse is
true, and that it is poetry which possesses the
greater and subtler power of evocation.   But the
language is, largely speaking, the same in both.
And consequently we must assume that this
superior quality of evocativeness or magic which
we associate with poetry has something to do with
the fact that, more artfully than in prose, the
language is *arranged*.   And this arrangement is,
obviously, in great part a matter of rhythm.

This brings us back, accordingly, to the afterthought in Wordsworth's appendix to the Lyrical Ballads—the idea that metre may impart "passion" to words. The truth of this seems irrefragable. When a poet, therefore, discards rhythm he is discarding perhaps the most powerful single *artifice* of poetry which is at his disposal— the particular artifice, moreover, which more than any other enables the poet to obtain a psychic control over his reader, to exert a sort of hypnosis over him. Rhythm is persuasive; it is the very stuff of life. It is not surprising therefore that things can be said in rhythm which otherwise cannot be said at all; paraphrase a fine passage of poetry into prose and in the dishevelment the ghost will have escaped. A good many champions of free verse would perhaps dispute this. They would fall back on the theory that, at any rate, certain moods more colloquial and less intense than those of the highest type of poetry, and less colloquial and more intense than those of the highest type of prose, could find their aptest expression in this form which lies halfway between. But even here their position will not be altogether secure, at least in theory. Is any contemporary poetry more colloquial or intimate than that of

FORD MADOX HUEFFER

T. S. Eliot, who is predominantly a metrical poet?
It is doubtful. Metrical verse, in other words,
can accomplish anything that free verse can, and
can do it more persuasively. What we inevitably come to is simply the fact that for some
poets free verse is an easier medium than metrical
verse, and consequently allows them greater efficiency. It is desirable therefore that such poets
should employ free verse. They only transgress
when they argue from this that free verse is the
finer form. This it is not.

The reasons for this would take us beyond the
mere question of rhythm. When Wordsworth
remarked that one could re-read with greater
pleasure a painful or tragic passage of poetry than
a similar passage of prose, although he mistakenly
ascribed this as altogether due to the presence of
metre, he nevertheless touched closely upon the
real principle at issue. For compared with the
pleasure derived from the reading of prose, the
pleasure of reading poetry is two-natured: in addition to the pleasure afforded by the ideas presented,
or the material (a pleasure which prose equally affords), there is also the more purely aesthetic delight of the art itself, a delight which might be de-

scribed as the sense of perfection in complexity, or the sense of arrangement. This arrangement is not solely a question of rhythm. It is also concerned with the selection of elements in the language more vividly sensuous and with the more adroit combination of ideas with a view to setting them off to sharper advantage. Given two poems in which the theme is equally delightful and effective on the first reading, that poem of the two which develops the theme with the richer and more perfect complexity of technique will longer afford pleasure in re-reading. It is, in other words, of more permanent value.

Mr. Hueffer confesses in advance that he prefers a less to a more complex form of art. As a matter of fact Mr. Hueffer is too modest. When he speaks of free verse he does not mean, to the extent in which it is usually meant, verse without rhythm. At his freest he is not far from a genuinely rhythmic method; and in many respects his sense of rhythm is both acute and individual. Three poems in his latest book would alone make it worth printing: "Antwerp," which is one of the three or four brilliant poems inspired by the war; "Foot-sloggers," which though not so good is none the less very readable; and "On Heaven," the poem which gives the volume its name. It is true that in all three of these poems Mr. Hueffer very often employs a rhythm which is almost as dispersed as that of prose; but the point to be emphatically remarked is that he does so only by way of variation on the given norm of movement, which is essentially and predominantly rhythmic. Variation of this sort is no more or less than good artistry; and Mr. Hueffer is a very competent artist, in whose hands even the most captious reader feels instinctively and at once secure. Does he at times overdo the dispersal of rhythm? Perhaps. There are moments, in "Antwerp" and in "On Heaven," when the relief of the reader on coming to a forcefully rhythmic passage is so marked as to make him suspect that the rhythm of the passage just left was not forceful enough. Mr. Hueffer is of a discursive temperament, viewed from whatever angle, and this leads him inevitably to over-inclusiveness and moments of let-down. One feels that a certain amount of cutting would improve both "Antwerp" and "On Heaven."

Yet one would hesitate to set about it oneself. Both poems are delightful. Mr. Hueffer writes with gusto and imagination, and—what is perhaps

rarer among contemporary poets—with tenderness. "On Heaven" may not be the very highest
type of poetry—it is clearly of the more colloquial
sort, delightfully expatiative, skilful in its use of
the more subdued tones of prose—but it takes hold
of one, and that is enough. One accepts it for
what it is, not demanding of it what the author
never intended to give it—that higher degree of
perfection in intricacy, that more intense and all-
fusing synthesis, which would have bestowed on
it the sort of beauty that more permanently
endures.

VI

The Literary Abbozzo: Lola Ridge

T HE Italians use the word *abbozzo*—meaning a sketch or unfinished work—not only in reference to drawing or painting but also as a sculptural term. The group of unfinished sculptures by Michelangelo in Florence, for example, takes this name; they are called simply *abbozzi*. The stone is still rough—the conception has only just begun to appear; it has not yet wholly or freely emerged. There is an impressiveness in the way in which the powerful figures seem struggling with the rock for release. And it is no wonder that Rodin and others have seen in this particular stage of a piece of sculpture a hint for a new method based on the clear enough aesthetic value of what might be called the provocatively incomplete.

Unfortunately, in literature as in sculpture, the

vogue of the incomplete has become too general, and has in consequence attracted many who are without a clear understanding of its principles. Two misconceptions regarding it are particularly common: one, that it is relatively formless, and therefore easier than a method more precise; the other, that it is a universal style, applicable to any one of the whole gamut of themes. Neither of these notions, of course, is true. The literary *abbozzo*—or to be more precise, the poetic *abbozzo* —demands a high degree of skill, a very sure instinct. And it should be equally apparent that it is properly applicable to what is relatively only a small number of moods or themes—among which one might place conspicuously the dithyrambic and the enumerative. These are moods which irregularity will often save from monotony. Whitman's catalogues would be even worse than they are had they been written as conscientiously in heroic couplets. The same is perhaps true of the dithyrambs of Ossian. Both poets to have been successful in a more skilfully elaborate style would have been compelled to delete a great deal . . . which would no doubt have been an improvement.

This makes one a little suspicious of the

abbozzo : is it possible that we overrate it a trifle? Might we not safely suggest to those artists whom we suspect of greatness, or even of very great skill merely, that their employment of the *abbozzo* should be chiefly as relaxation? But they will hardly need to be told. The provocatively incomplete—which is to be sharply distinguished from the merely truncated or slovenly—has its charm, its beautiful suggestiveness; but in proportion as the artist is powerful he will find the *abbozzo* insufficient, he will want to substitute for this charm, this delicate hover, a beauty and strength more palpable. The charm which inheres in the implied rather than the explicit he knows how to retain—he will retain it in the dim counterpoint of thought itself.

The poems of Miss Lola Ridge raise all these issues sharply, no less because the author has richness and originality of sensibility, and at times brilliance of idea, than because she follows this now too common vogue Here is a vivid personality, even a powerful one, clearly aware of the peculiar experience which is its own—a not too frequent gift. It rejoices in the streaming and garishly lighted multiplicity of the city: it turns eagerly toward the semi-tropical fecundity of the

meaner streets and tenement districts. Here it is
the human item that most attracts Miss Ridge—
Jews, for the most part, seen darkly and warmly
against a background of social consciousness, of
rebelliousness even. She arranges her figures for
us with a muscular force which seems masculine;
it is singular to come upon a book written by a
woman in which vigour is so clearly a more natural
quality than grace. This is sometimes merely
strident, it is true. When she compares Time to
a paralytic, "A mildewed hulk above the nations
squatting," one fails to respond. Nor is one
moved precisely as Miss Ridge might hope when
she tells us of a wind which "noses among them
like a skunk that roots about the heart." It is
apparent from the frequency with which such
falsities occur—particularly in the section called
"Labour"—that Miss Ridge is a trifle obsessed
with the concern of being powerful: she forgets
that the harsh is only harsh when used sparingly,
the loud only loud when it emerges from the quiet.
She is uncertain enough of herself to deal in harsh-
nesses wholesale and to scream them.

But with due allowances made for these extravagances—the extravagances of the brilliant but
somewhat too abounding amateur—one must pay

one's respects to Miss Ridge for her very frequent
verbal felicities, for her images brightly lighted,
for a few shorter poems which are clusters of
glittering phrases, and for the human richness of
one longer poem, "The Ghetto," in which the
vigorous and the tender are admirably fused.
Here Miss Ridge's reactions are fullest and
truest. Here she is under no compulsion to be
strident. And it is precisely because here she is
relatively most successful that one is most awk-
wardly conscious of the defects inherent in the
whole method for which Miss Ridge stands.
This is a use of the "provocatively incomplete"—
as concerns form—in which, unfortunately, the
provocative has been left out. If we consider
again, for a moment, Michelangelo's *abbozzi*, we
become aware how slightly, by comparison, Miss
Ridge's figures have begun to emerge. Have they
emerged enough to suggest the clear overtone of
the thing completed? The charm of the incomplete is of course in its positing of a norm which
it suggests, approaches, retreats from, or at points
actually touches. The ghost of completeness
alternately shines and dims. But for Miss Ridge
these subtleties of form do not come forward.
She is content to use for the most part a direct

prose, with only seldom an interpellation of the metrical, and the metrical of a not particularly skilful sort. The latent harmonies are never evoked.

One hesitates to make suggestions. Miss Ridge might have to sacrifice too much vigour and richness to obtain a greater beauty of form: the effort might prove her undoing. By the degree of her success or failure in this undertaking, however, she would become aware of her real capacities as an artist. Or is she wise enough to know beforehand that the effort would be fruitless, and that she has already reached what is for her the right pitch? That would be a confession but it would leave us, even so, a wide margin for gratitude.

VII

The Melodic Line: D. H. Lawrence

IT has been said that all the arts are constantly attempting, within their respective spheres, to attain to something of the quality of music, to assume, whether in pigment, or pencil, or marble, or prose, something of its speed and flash, emotional completeness, and well-harmonied resonance; but of no other single art is that so characteristically or persistently true as it is of poetry. Poetry is indeed in this regard two-natured: it strikes us, when it is at its best, quite as sharply through our sense of the musically beautiful as through whatever implications it has to carry of thought or feeling: it plays on us alternately or simultaneously through sound as well as through sense. The writers of free verse have demonstrated, to be sure, that a poetry sufficiently effective may be written in almost entire disregard of the values of pure rhythm. The poetry of "H.D." is perhaps the clearest example of this. Severe concentration upon a damascene sharpness of sense-impression, a stripping of images to the white clear kernel, both of which matters can be more meticulously attended to if there are no bafflements of rhythm or rhyme-pattern to be contended with, have, to a considerable extent, a substitutional value. Such a poetry attains a vitreous lucidity which has its own odd heatless charm. But a part of its charm lies in its very act of departure from a norm which, like a background or undertone, is forever present for it in our minds; we like it in a sense because of its unique perversity as a variation on this more familiar order of rhythmic and harmonic suspensions and resolutions; we like it in short for its novelty; and it eventually leaves us unsatisfied, because this more familiar order is based on a musical hunger which is as profound and permanent as it is universal.

When we read a poem we are aware of this musical characteristic, or analogy, in several ways. The poem as a whole in this regard will satisfy us or not in accordance with the presence, or partial presence, or absence, of what we might term musical unity. The "Ode to a Nightingale" is an example of perfect musical unity; the "Ode to Autumn" is an example of partial musical unity,—partial because the resolution comes too soon, the rate of curve is too abruptly altered; many of the poems by contemporary writers of free verse—Fletcher, or Aldington, or "H.D."—illustrate what we mean by lack of musical unity or integration, except on the secondary plane, the plane of what we might call orotundity; and the most complete lack of all may be found in the vast majority of Whitman's poems. This particular sort of musical quality in poetry is, however, so nearly identifiable with the architectural as to be hardly separable from it. It is usually in the briefer movements of a poem that musical charm is most keenly felt. And this sort of brief and intensely satisfactory musical movement we might well describe as something closely analogous to what is called in musical compositions the melodic line.

By melodic line we shall not mean to limit ourselves to one line of verse merely. Our melodic line may be, indeed, one line of verse, or half a line, or a group of lines, or half a page. What we have in mind is that sort of brief movement when, for whatever psychological reason, there is suddenly a fusion of all the many qualities, which may by themselves constitute charm, into one indivisible magic. Is it possible for this psychological change to take place without entailing an immediate heightening of rhythmic effect? Possible, perhaps, but extremely unlikely. In a free verse poem we shall expect to see at such moments a very much closer approximation to the rhythm of metrical verse: in a metrical poem we shall expect to see a subtilization of metrical effects, a richer or finer employment of vowel and consonantal changes to that end. Isolate such a passage in a free verse poem or metrical poem and it will be seen how true this is. The change is immediately perceptible, like the change from a voice talking to a voice singing. The change is as profound in time as it is in tone, yet it is one which escapes any but the most superficial analysis. All we can say of it is that it at once alters the character of the verse we are reading from that sort which pleases and is forgotten, pleases without disturbing, to that sort which strikes into the subconscious, gleams, and is automatically remembered. In the midst of the rich semi-prose recitative of Fletcher's White Symphony, for ex-

ample, a recitative which charms and entices but
does not quite enchant, or take one's memory, one
comes to the following passage:

> Autumn! Golden fountains,
> And the winds neighing
> Amid the monotonous hills;
> Desolation of the old gods,
> Rain that lifts and rain that moves away;
> In the green-black torrent
> Scarlet leaves.

It is an interlude of song and one remembers it.
Is this due to an intensification of rhythm?
Partly, no doubt, but not altogether. The emotional heightening is just as clear, and the unity
of impression is pronounced; it is a fusion of all
these qualities, and it is impossible to say which
is the primum mobile. As objective psychologists all we can conclude is that in what is conspicuously a magical passage in this poem there is
a conspicuous increase in the persuasiveness of
rhythm.

This is equally true of metrical poetry. It is
these passages of iridescent fusion that we recall
from among the many thousands of lines we have
read. One has but to summon up from one's
memory the odds and ends of poems which willy

SCEPTICISMS

nilly one remembers, precious fragments cherished
by the jackdaw of the subconscious:

A savage spot as holy and enchanted
As e'er beneath a waning moon was haunted
By woman wailing for her demon-lover.

I have seen them riding seaward on the waves
Combing the white hair of the waves blown back
When the wind blows the water white and black.

Beauty is momentary in the mind,—
The fitful tracing of a portal:
But in the flesh it is immortal.

And shook a most divine dance from their feet,
That twinkled starlike, moved as swift, and fine,
And beat the air so thin, they made it shine.

Part of a moon was falling down the west
Dragging the whole sky with it to the hills.
Its light poured softly in her lap.   She saw
And spread her apron to it.   She put out her hand
Among the harp-like morning-glory strings,
Taut with the dew from garden-bed to eaves,
As if she played unheard the tenderness
That wrought on him. . . .

Awakening up, he took her hollow lute,—
Tumultuous,—and in chords that tenderest be,

D. H. LAWRENCE

He played an ancient ditty long since mute,
In Provence called, "La Belle Dame Sans Merci."

Ay, Mother, Mother,
What is this Man, thy darling kissed and cuffed,
Thou lustingly engenders't,
To sweat, and make his brag, and rot,
Crowned with all honours and all shamefulness?
He dogs the secret footsteps of the heavens,
Sifts in his hands the stars, weighs them as gold-dust,
And yet is he successive unto nothing,
But patrimony of a little mould,
And entail of four planks.

And suddenly there's no meaning in our kiss,
And your lit upward face grows, where we lie,
Lonelier and dreadfuller than sunlight is,
And dumb and mad and eyeless like the sky.

All of these excerpts, mangled as they are by
being hewed from their contexts, have in a notice-
able degree the quality of the "melodic line."
They are the moments for which, indeed, we read
poetry; just as when in listening to a modern music
however complex and dissonantal, it is after all
the occasionally-arising brief cry of lyricism which
thrills and dissolves us. When the subconscious
speaks, the subconscious answers.

It is because in a good deal of contemporary

poetry the importance of the melodic line is forgotten that this brief survey has been made. In our preoccupations with the many technical quarrels, and quarrels as to aesthetic purpose, which have latterly embroiled our poets, we have, I think, a little lost sight of the fact that poetry to be poetry must after all rise above a mere efficiency of charmingness, or efficiency of accuracy, to this sort of piercing perfection of beauty or truth, phrased in a piercing perfection of music. It is a wholesome thing for us to study the uses of dissonance and irregularity; we add in that way, whether sensuously or psychologically, many new tones; but there is danger that the habit will grow upon us, that we will forget the reasons for our adoption of these qualities and use them *passim* and without intelligence, or, as critics, confer a too arbitrary value upon them.

The poetry of Mr. D. H. Lawrence is a case very much in point. His temperament is modern to a degree: morbidly self-conscious, sex-crucified, an affair of stretched and twanging nerves. He belongs, of course, to the psychological wing of modern poetry. Although we first met him as an Imagist, it is rather with T. S. Eliot, or Masters, or the much gentler Robinson, all of whom are in a

D . H . LAWRENCE

sense lineal descendants of the Meredith of
"Modern Love," that he belongs. But he does
not much resemble any of these. His range is
extremely narrow,—it is nearly always erotic,
febrile and sultry at the lower end, plangently
philosophic at the upper. Within this range he
is astonishingly various. No mood is too slight
to be seized upon, to be thrust under his myopic
lens. Here, in fact, we touch his cardinal weakness: for if as a novelist he often writes like a
poet, as a poet he far too often writes like a
novelist. One observes that he knows this himself—he asks the reader of "Look! We Have
Come Through!" to consider it not as a collection of short poems, but as a sort of novel
in verse. No great rearrangement, perhaps,
would have been necessary to do the same thing
for "New Poems" or "Amores," though perhaps
not so cogently. More than most poets he makes
of his poetry a sequential, though somewhat disjointed, autobiography. And more than almost
any poet one can think of, who compares with
him for richness of temperament, he is unselective
in doing so, both as to material and method.

He is, indeed, as striking an example as one
could find of the poet who, while appearing to be

capable of what we have called the melodic line, none the less seems to be unaware of the value and importance of it, and gives it to us at random, brokenly, half blindly, or intermingled with splintered fragments of obscure sensation and extraneous detail dragged in to fill out a line. A provoking poet! and a fatiguing one: a poet of the dæmonic type, a man possessed, who is swept helplessly struggling and lashing down the black torrent of his thought; alternately frenzied and resigned. "A poet," says Santayana, "who merely swam out into the sea of sensibility, and tried to picture all possible things . . . would bring materials only to the workshop of art; he would not be an artist." What Santayana had in mind was a poet who undertook this with a deliberateness—but the effect in the case of Mr. Lawrence is much the same. He is seldom wholly an artist, even when his medium is most under control. It is when he is at his coolest, often,—when he tries rhyme-pattern or rhythm-pattern or colour-pattern in an attempt at the sort of icy kaleidoscopics at which Miss Lowell is adept,—that he is most tortuously and harshly and artificially and altogether unreadably at his worst. Is he obsessed with dissonance and oddity? It would seem so.

D. H. LAWRENCE

His rhymes are cruel, sometimes, to the verge of murder.

Yet, if he is not wholly an artist, he is certainly, in at least a fragmentary sense, a brilliant poet. Even that is hardly fair enough: the two more recent volumes contain more than a handful of uniquely captivating poems. They have a curious quality,—tawny, stark, bitter, harshly coloured, salt to the taste. The sadistic element in them is strong. It is usually in the love poems that he is best: in these he is closest to giving us the melodic line that comes out clear and singing. Closest indeed; but the perfect achievement is seldom. The fusion is not complete. The rhythms do not altogether free themselves, one feels that they are weighted; the impressions are impetuously crowded and huddled; and as concerns the commanding of words Mr. Lawrence is a captain of more force than tact: he is obeyed, but sullenly. Part of this is due, no doubt, to Mr. Lawrence's venturings among moods and sensations which no poet has hitherto attempted, moods secret and obscure, shadowy and suspicious. This is to his credit, and greatly to the credit of poetry. He is among the most original poets of our time, original, that is, as regards sensibility; he has given us sombre and macabre tones, and tones of a cold and sinister clarity, or of a steely passion, which we have not had before. His nerves are raw, his reactions are idiosyncratic: what is clear enough to him has sometimes an unhealthily mottled look to us,—esuriently etched, none the less. But a great deal of the time he over-reaches: he makes frequently the mistake of, precisely, trying too hard. What cannot be captured, in this regard, it is no use killing. Brutality is no substitute for magic. One must take one's mood alive and sing-ing, or not at all.

It is this factor which in the poetry of Mr. Lawrence most persistently operates to prevent the attainment of the perfect melodic line. Again and again he gives us a sort of jagged and spangled flame; but the mood does not sing quite with the naturalness or ease one would hope for, it has the air of being dazed by violence, or even seems, in the very act of singing, to bleed a little. It is a trifle too easy to say of a poet of whom this is true that the fault may be due to an obtrusion of the intellect among the emotions. Such terms do not define, are scarcely separable. Perhaps it would more closely indicate the difficulty to say that Mr. Lawrence is not only, as all poets are, a curious blending of the psycho-analyst and patient, but that he endeavours to carry on both rôles at once, to speak with both voices simultaneously. The soliloquy of the patient—the lyricism of the subconscious—is for ever being broken in upon by the too eager inquisitions of the analyst. If Mr. Lawrence could make up his mind to yield the floor unreservedly to either, he would be on the one hand a clearer and more magical poet, on the other hand a more dependable realist.

One wonders, in the upshot, whether the theme of "Look! We have Come Through!" had better not have been treated in prose. The story, such as it is, emerges, it is true, and with many deliciously clear moments, some of them lyric and piercing; but with a good deal that remains in question. It is the poet writing very much as a novelist, and all too often forgetting that the passage from the novel to the poem is among other things a passage from the cumulative to the selective. Sensations and impressions may be hewed and hauled in prose; but in poetry it is rather the sort of mood which, like a bird, flies out of the tree as soon as the ax rings against it, that one must look for. Mr. Lawrence has, of this sort, his birds, but he appears to pay little heed to them; he goes on chopping. And one has, even so, such a delight in him that not for worlds would one intervene.

VIII

Possessor and Possessed: John Gould Fletcher

THE work of Mr. John Gould Fletcher has hardly attained the eminence in contemporary poetry that it deserves. One is doubtful, indeed, whether it will. For not only is it of that sort which inevitably attracts only a small audience, but it is also singularly uneven in quality, and many readers who would like Mr. Fletcher at his best cannot muster the patience to read beyond his worst. Mr. Fletcher is his own implacable enemy. He has not yet published a book in which his excellent qualities are single, candid, and undivided: a great many dead leaves are always to be turned. The reward for the search is conspicuous, but unfortunately it is one which few will take the trouble to find.

Mr. Fletcher's latest book, "The Tree of Life" is no exception to this rule: it is perhaps. if we leave

out of account his five early books of orthodox
and nugatory self-exploration, the most remarkably uneven of them all. It has neither the level
technical excellence, the economical terseness of
his "Japanese Prints," nor, on the other hand, the
amazing flight of many pages in "Goblins and
Pagodas." Yet certainly one would rather have
it than "Japanese Prints"; and even if it contains a
greater proportion of dross than is to be found in
the symphonies, it has compensating qualities,
qualities which one feels are new in the work of
Mr. Fletcher, and which make one hesitate to rate
it too far below "Goblins and Pagodas," or, at any
rate, "Irradiations." For the moment, however, it
is interesting to set aside these new qualities and
to consider, or savour, the astonishing unequalness
which alone would constitute a sort of distinction
in the work of Mr. Fletcher. It is the custom in
such cases to say that the poet has no self-critical
faculty, and to let it go at that. But that explanation is of a general and vague character, and
operates only under the fallacy that any such complex is reducible to the terms of a single factor.
It should be clear that any given complex will
consist of several factors; that "absence of a critical faculty" is to a considerable degree a merely

negative diagnosis; and that perhaps one would wisely look for a more express clue to the particular personal equation in something more positive—as for example in some excess rather than lack. It is in a kind of redundancy, on the psychic plane, that an artist's character is most manifest. Here will lie the key to both his successes and his failures. It should be the critic's undertaking to name and analyse this redundancy and to ascertain the degree in which the artist has it under control.

Unfortunately, this undertaking, in the present state of psychology—and criticism is a branch of psychology—is as yet highly speculative; it borders, indeed, in the opinion of many, on the mythological. Criticism of this sort must be, confessedly, supposititious. Thus in the case of Mr. Fletcher we shall perhaps find the most suggestive light cast from a direction which to many literary folk is highly suspect—from psychology itself. Kostyleff, it will be recalled, maintains that a very important part of the mechanism of poetic inspiration rests in the automatic discharge of verbal reflexes—the initial impulse coming from some external stimulus, but the chain of verbal association thereafter unravelling more or less of its own momentum, and leading, as far as any connection of thought or emotion is concerned, well beyond the premises of the original stimulus. Of course Kostyleff does not limit himself to this. He grants that it is only a peculiar sensibility which will store up, as in the case of a poet, such a wealth of verbal reflexes: and he grants further that there is often—though not always—the initial stimulus from without. For our part, as soon as we apply this engaging theory to the work of poets, we see that certain aspects of it are more illuminating in some cases than others; in other words, that while the principle as a whole is true of all poets, in some poets it is one factor which is more important, and in some another. It is true, for example, that Mr. Fletcher has a very original sensibility, and it is also true that his initial stimulus sometimes comes from without, but whereas in the work of certain other poets these factors might be paramount, in the case of Mr. Fletcher the striking feature has always been his habit of surrendering himself, almost completely, to the power of these automatically, unravelling verbal reflexes. In fact the poetry of Mr. Fletcher is as remarkable an illustration of this principle as one could find.

JOHN GOULD FLETCHER

The implications are rich. What occurs to one immediately is that, as the functioning of these verbal reflexes is most rapid when least consciously controlled, the poet will be at his best when the initial stimulus is of a nature to leave him greatest freedom. To such a poet, it will be seen, it would be a great handicap, to have to adhere too closely, throughout a longish poem, to a fixed and unalterable idea. The best theme for him will be the one which is least definite, one which will start him off at top speed but will be rather enhanced than impaired by the introduction and development of new elements, by rapid successive improvisations in unforeseen directions. Any sort of conceptual framework prepared in advance with regard either to subject or form would be perpetually retarding him, perpetually bringing him back to a more severely conscious plane of effort, a plane on which, the chances are, he would be far less effective. These suppositions gain force when we turn, in their light, to Mr. Fletcher's work. In "Irradiations" we find him taking his first ecstatic plunge into improvisation—formalism is thrown to the winds, and with it much which for this poet perplexes and retards; and an amazingly rich treasure house of verbal reflexes, the gift of a

temperament almost hyperaesthetic in its sensitiveness to colour, line, and texture—a temperament in
which some profound disharmony is most easily
struck at and shaken through these senses—is for
the first time rifled.   It is in this stage of a lyric
poet's career that his speech most glistens.   Impressions come up shining from their long burial
in the subconscious.   The poet is perhaps a little
breathless with his sudden wealth—he is at first
content to bring up only small handfuls of the
most glittering coin; he is even perhaps a little
distrustful of it.   But the habit of allowing himself to be possessed by this wealth grows rapidly.
The mechanism becomes more familiar, if anything so vague as this kind of apperception can be
said to be truly recognizable, and the poet learns
the trick of shutting his eyes and not merely allowing, but precisely inviting, his subconscious to take
possession of him.   The trick consists largely in a
knowledge, abruptly acquired, of his own character, and of such ideas as are, therefore, the
"Open Sesame!" to this cave.   It was in colourism
that Mr. Fletcher found this password.   And it
was in "Goblins and Pagodas" that he first put it
to full and gorgeous use.

   For in the idea of a series of symphonies in

which the sole unity was to be a harmony of colour, in which form and emotional tone could follow the lead of colouristic word-associations no matter how far afield, Mr. Fletcher discovered an "Open Sesame!" so ideal to his nature, and so powerful, as not merely to open the door, but at one stroke to lay bare his treasure entire. One should not overlook here also an important secondary element in Mr. Fletcher's nature, a strong but partial affinity for musical construction, a feeling for powerful submerged rhythms less ordered than those of metrical verse, but more ordered than those of prose; and this element, too, found its ideal opportunity in the colour symphonies. The result was, naturally, the most brilliant and powerful work which Mr. Fletcher has yet given us—a poetry unlike any other. It contains no thought: Mr. Fletcher is not a conceptual poet. It contains, in the strictly human sense, extraordinarily little of the sort of emotion which relates to the daily life of men and women; there are despairs and exaltations and sorrows and hopes, and the furious energy of ambition, and the weariness of resignation, but they are the emotions of someone incorporeal, and their sphere of action is among winds and clouds, the colours of sky and sea, the glittering of rain and jewels, and not among the perplexed hearts of humanity. In a sense it is like the symbolism of such poets as Mallarmé, but with the difference that here the symbols have no meaning. It is a sort of absolute poetry, a poetry of detached waver and brilliance, a beautiful flowering of language alone, a parthenogenesis, as if language were fertilized by itself rather than by thought or feeling. Remove the magic of phrase and sound, and there is nothing left: no thread of continuity, no relation between one page and the next, no thought, no story, no emotion. But the magic of phrase and sound is powerful, and it takes one into a fantastic world where one is etherealized, where one has deep emotions indeed, but emotions star-powdered, and blown to flame by speed and intensity rather than by thought or human warmth.

Unfortunately it is only for a little while that a poet can be so completely possessed by the subconscious: the more complete the possession the more rapid the exhaustion. One or two of Mr. Fletcher's colour symphonies showed already a flagging of energy, and in addition to the unevenness which is inevitable in a blind obedience to the lead of word-association alone (since it leads as often to verbosity as to magic) that unevenness also is noticed which comes of the poet's attempt to substitute the consciously for the unconsciously found—an attempt which for such a temperament as Mr. Fletcher's is frequently doomed to failure. There are limits, moreover, as we have seen, to the number of themes which will draw out the best of the possessed type of poet. . Failing to discover new themes, he must repeat the old ones; and here it is not long before he feels his consciousness intruding, and saying to him, "You have said this before," a consciousness which at once inhibits the unravelling of word-association, and brings him back to that more deliberate sort of art for which he is not so well fitted. It is to this point that Mr. Fletcher has come, recently in "Japanese Prints," and now in "The Tree of Life." Here and there for a moment is a flash of magic and power—there are pages, even whole poems, which are only less delightful than the symphonies —but intermingled with how much that is lame, stiltedly metrical, verbose, or downright ugly. The use of regular metre or rhyme brings him down with a thud. . . . "The Tree of Life" is a volume of love poems, more personal than Mr. Fletcher has given us hitherto, and that has an interest of its own. But the colourism has begun to dim, it is often merely a wordy and tediously overcrowded imitation of the coloured swiftness of "Goblins and Pagodas," the images indistinct and conflicting; and if one is to hope for further brilliance it is not in this but in a new note, audible here and there in the shorter lyrics, a note of iron-like resonance, bitterly personal, and written in a free verse akin to the stark eloquence of Biblical prose. . . . Are these lyrics an earnest of further development, and will Mr. Fletcher pass to that other plane of art, that of the possessor artist, the artist who foresees and forges, who calculates his effects? There is hardly enough evidence here to make one sure.

IX

The Technique of Polyphonic Prose: Amy Lowell

MISS LOWELL can always be delightfully counted upon to furnish us with something of a literary novelty. She has a genius for vivifying theory. No sooner, for example, had she uttered the words "Free verse!" (which previously in the mouth of Mr. Pound had left us cold) than we closed about them as a crowd closes upon an accident, in a passion of curiosity; and if ultimately some of us were a little disappointed with the theory more shrewdly inspected, we could be thankful at least that it had left us Miss Lowell's poems. So now, with the publication of "Can Grande's Castle"—"four modern epics," as the publishers term them—Miss Lowell bids fair to stampede us anew under the banner of "polyphonic prose." This is an astonishing book; never was Miss Lowell's sheer energy of mind more in evidence. Viewed simply as a piece of verbal craftsmanship it is a sort of Roget's Thesaurus of colour. Viewed as a piece of historical reconstruction it is a remarkable feat of documentation, particularly the longest of the "epics," the story of the bronze horses of San Marco. Viewed as poetry, or prose, or polyphonic prose—or let us say, for caution's sake, as literature—well, that is another question. It is a tribute to Miss Lowell's fecundity of mind that one must react to her four prose-poems in so great a variety of ways.

Miss Lowell has always been outspokenly a champion of the theory that a large part of an artist's equipment is hard work, patient and unimpassioned craftsmanship. This is true, and Miss Lowell's own poetry can always be counted upon to display, within its known and unchangeable limitations, a verbal, an aesthetic, and even, at moments, a metrical craftsmanship, of a high order. Whether viewed technically or not, her work is always, and particularly to an artist, intriguing and suggestive: this much one can safely say in advance. When we begin, however, to assume toward her work that attitude which consists in an attempt to see the contemporary as later, through the perspective of time, it will appear to posterity, we change our ground somewhat. Novelty must be discounted; and exquisite tool-work must be seen not as if through the microscope but in its properly ancillary position as a contributing element in the artist's total success or failure. This is in effect to judge as we can of the artist's sensibility and mental character—not an easy thing to do. The judge must see over the walls of his own personality. Fortunately, aesthetic judgment is not entirely solipsistic, but is in part guided by certain aesthetic laws, vague but none the less usable.

Miss Lowell asserts in her preface that polyphonic prose is not an order of prose. Let us not quarrel with her on this point. The important questions are: first, its possible effectiveness as an art form; and second, its effectiveness as employed through the temperament of Miss Lowell. She says:

Metrical verse has one set of laws, cadenced verse another, polyphonic prose can go from one to the other in the same poem with no sense of incongruity. Its only touchstone is the taste and feeling of its author. . . . Yet, like all other artistic forms, it has certain fundamental principles, and the chief of these is an insistence on the absolute adequacy of a passage to the thought it embodies. Taste is therefore its determining factor; taste and a rhythmic ear.

But all this is merely equivalent to saying that any expression of the artist is inevitably self-expression, as if one "threw the nerves in patterns on a screen." The real touchstone of a work of art is not, ultimately, the taste or feeling of the author (a singularly unreliable judge) but the degree to which it "gets across," (as they say of the drama) to, let us say, an intelligent audience.

And here one may properly question whether in their totality Miss Lowell's prose-poems quite "get across." They are brilliant, in the aesthetic sense; they are amazingly rich and frequently delightful in incident; they are unflaggingly visualized; they are, in a manner, triumphs of co-ordination. And yet, they do not quite come off. Why is this? Is it the fault of Miss Lowell or of the form? A little of each; and the reasons are many. Of the more obvious sort is the simple but deadly fact that without exception these four prose-poems are too long. Not too long in an absolute sense, for that would be ridiculous, but too long, first, in relation to the amount and nature of the narrative element in them, and second, in relation to the

manner, or style, in which they are written. Parallels are not easy to find; but one can perhaps not
outrageously adduce Flaubert's "Herodias" and
"Salammbo" as examples of success in what is very
much the same, not form, but tone of art. Miss
Lowell, like Flaubert, attempts a very vivid and
heavily laden reconstruction of striking historical
events. No item is too small to be recreated for
its effect in producing a living and sensuous
veridity. But there are two important differences.
In Flaubert this living sensuousness is nearly always subordinated to the narrative, is indeed
merely the background for it; whereas for Miss
Lowell this sensuous reconstruction is perhaps the
main intention. And furthermore, whereas Flaubert employed a prose of which the chief purpose
was that it should be unobtrusively a vehicle, Miss
Lowell employs a prose bristlingly self-conscious,
of which an important purpose is stylistic and
colouristic brilliance.

The defects that arise from these two differences
are very serious. They combine to rob Miss
Lowell of the fruits to which sheer adroitness of
craftsmanship might otherwise have entitled her.
Put briefly, these poems are over-descriptive.
When one considers their length, the narrative

element is much too slight; and not only that, it is too disjointed. Narrative description, even though able, is not enough. In "Sea-Blue and Blood-Red" Miss Lowell introduces a really narrative theme—narrative, that is, in the sense that it involves real *dramatis personae*, in the persons of Nelson and Lady Hamilton—and in consequence the reader's interest is a good deal better held. It would be still better held however if the protagonists had been conceived less as gaudily sheathed mannequins, gesticulating feverishly in a whirl of coloured lights and confetti, and more as human beings. It is intended to show them as puppets, of course, but that effect would hardly have been diminished by making them psychologically more appealing. In "Hedge Island," "Guns as Keys," and "Bronze Horses" the unifying themes are still more tenuous: the supersession of the stagecoach by the train, Commodore Perry's voyage to Japan, the travels of the four horses of San Marco. All of them are acute studies of societal change. One feels in all of them the impressiveness of the conception, but in the actual execution the impressiveness has partially escaped. One is, in fact, less often impressed than fatigued.

And this fatigue, as above intimated, is due not

merely to the lack of humanly interesting narrative (as would be added by the introduction of a character or group of characters who should enlist our sympathies throughout) but also to the nature of the style which Miss Lowell uses. For here Miss Lowell, led astray by love of experiment, has made, in the opinion of the present reviewer, a series of fundamental errors. The style she has chosen to use, whether regarded with a view to rhythm or to colour-distribution, is essentially pointillistic. Now Miss Lowell should have known that the pointillistic style is, in literature, suited only to very brief movements. A short poem based on this method may be brilliantly successful; Miss Lowell has herself proved it. A long poem based on this method, even though sustainedly brilliant, and perhaps in direct ratio to its brilliance, almost inevitably becomes dull. In her preface Miss Lowell says that she has taken for the basis of her rhythm the long cadence of oratorical prose. In this however she is mistaken. She has an inveterate and profoundly temperamental and hence perhaps unalterable addiction to a short, ejaculatory, and abrupt style—a style indeed of which the most striking merits and defects are its vigorous curtness and its almost total lack of curve and grace. This is true of her work whether in metrical verse, free verse, or prose; it is as true of "The Cremona Violin" as of "The Bombardment." This style, obviously, is ideal for a moment of rapid action or extreme emotional intensity. But its effect when used *passim* is not only fatiguing, it is actually irritating. Its pace is too often out of all proportion to the pace of the action. One feels like a horse who is at the same time whipped up and reined in. The restlessness is perpetual, there is no hope of relaxation or ease, one longs in vain for a slowing down of the movement, an expansion of it into longer and more languid waves. One longs, too, for that delicious sublimation of tranquillity and pause which comes of a beautiful transition from the exclamatory to the contemplative, from the rigidly angular to the musically curved.

This misapplication of style to theme manifests itself as clearly on the narrowly aesthetic plane as on the rhythmic. Here again one sees a misuse of pointillism, for Miss Lowell splashes too much colour, uses colour and vivid image too unrestrainedly and too much at the same pitch of intensity. The result is that the rate of aesthetic fatigue on the reader's part is relatively rapid. So persistent is

Miss Lowell's colouristic attitude, so nearly un-varied is her habit of presenting people, things, and events in terms of colour alone, that presently she has reduced one to a state of colour blindness. Image kills image, hue obliterates hue, one page erases another. And when this point has been reached one realizes that Miss Lowell's polyphonic prose has little else to offer. Its sole *raison d'être* is its vividness.

One wonders, indeed, whether Miss Lowell has not overestimated the possibilities of this form. It is precisely at those points where polyphonic prose is more self-conscious or artificial than or-dinary prose—where it introduces an excess of rhyme, assonance, and alliteration—that it is most markedly inferior to it. Theory to the con-trary, these shifts from prose to wingèd prose or verse are often so abrupt as to be incongruous and disturbing. But disturbance as an element in aesthetic attack should be subordinate, not domi-nant—the exception, not the rule. Miss Lowell's polyphonic prose is a perpetual furor of disturb-ance, both of thought and of style. Again, re-frain should be sparely used, adroitly varied and concealed; and the counterpoint of thought, if it is not to become monotonous, must be a good deal subtler than it is, for instance, in "Bronze Horses." All these artifices are used to excess, and the up- shot is a style of which the most salient character- istic is exuberance without charm. "Taste" and "rhythmic ear" too frequently fail. And one is merely amused when one encounters a passage like the following:

Such a pounding, pummelling, pitching, pointing, pierc- ing, pushing, pelting, poking, panting, punching, parry- ing, pulling, prodding, puking, piling, passing, you never did see.

It is hard to regard this as anything but tyronism.

These are the main features of the artistic in- completeness of "Can Grande's Castle." One could analyse it further, of course—one thinks, for example, of Miss Lowell's habit, when tempted to use a simile, of comparing the larger thing to the smaller, as the sea or the sky to a flower; the effect of which is not at all what is intended, and very unpleasant. A simile may be successful in point of colour, and yet fail because of its ineptitude on another plane, as by suggesting rigidity when liquidity is desired, or minuteness when it is desired to suggest spaciousness. But this is ele- mentary, a minor point, and it is time to return to our starting place, and to reiterate what has perhaps in this prolonged analysis been lost sight of; namely, that even what is relatively a failure for Miss Lowell is none the less brilliant, and would suffice to make the reputation of a lesser poet. "Can Grande's Castle" is a remarkable book, a book which every one interested in the direction of contemporary poetry should read, whether for its own sake or for its value as the test of a new form of art.

X

Poetry as Supernaturalism: William Stanley Braithwaite

THE energy of Mr. Braithwaite is unflagging. Not content with bringing out annually the "Anthology of Magazine Verse," he has lately entered upon another and even huger enterprise—"A Critical Anthology," he calls it; and this, too, threatens to become a hardy perennial. In these four hundred pages, which for the greater part consist of his reviews in the Boston *Evening Transcript*, slightly revised and cast into the form of *al fresco* conversations between Mr. Braithwaite and three others, Mr. Braithwaite purports to cover the entire field of English and American poetry for 1916. Some fifty odd poets are discussed here, a list long enough surely to have included certain poets whose omission seems singular enough to warrant a more specific explanation than Mr. Braithwaite offers.

WILLIAM BRAITHWAITE

Mr. Robert Frost and Mr. Wilfrid Wilson Gibson come in for only incidental mention. Messrs. Wallace Stevens, T. S. Eliot, and Maxwell Bodenheim (whose work has appeared in anthologies) are not mentioned at all. With these exceptions, however, the list is complete enough to afford us a clear idea of Mr. Braithwaite's temper and method.

Concerning his predilections, Mr. Braithwaite leaves us in no doubt whatever. At the very centre of his attitude toward poetry is the express belief that poetry is a sort of supernaturalism. "It is the sacerdotal wonder of life which poets feel," he remarks. "More certainly than other men, poets are conscious of pre-existence, in other worlds, and in this too." Elsewhere, one encounters also such expressions as "reverence for life," "quest for beauty," and "mystic illumination." This sort of thing, one must confess, is a little too easy. Is it not really a shrugging of the critic's burden from his own shoulders,—onto the shoulders of God? This is no place, to be sure, for a quarrel over the importance or the reality of God; but it is perhaps not going too far to say that within the sphere of man's consciousness, no matter to what miraculous origin it be ascribed, all things are at least subject to man's observation and analysis. If in the presence of a piece of poetry the critic is content merely with the exclamatory, he is not doing his work. Let him remember that he is dealing, at least in large measure, not with the supernatural but with the natural; and what is natural has natural (biological and psychological) causes. These it is the critic's duty to determine and to relate.

It is easy to see, therefore, where, in his relation to contemporary poetry, so fundamental a failure leads Mr. Braithwaite. With this somewhat quaint notion of the holiness of poetry in his head it is natural that he should be most tolerant toward that sort of poetry which itself, in somewhat the same manner, takes for granted the not-to-be-questioned holiness of life. In his present book, therefore, Mr. Braithwaite puts a clear emotional emphasis on work which is characteristically sentimental. Lizette Woodworth Reese, Bliss Carman, Amelia Josephine Burr, Olive Tilford Dargan, Louis V. Ledoux, Hermann Hagedorn,—these are some of the poets about whom Mr. Braithwaite can talk with unrestrained enthusiasm. They, and to a less extent Edwin Arlington Robinson, observe toward life, in varying degrees, an attitude of chaste, romantic awe; and it is this attitude, particularly when it approaches the sweetly ecstatic or appears to be barely concealing a sob, that most delights Mr. Braithwaite. Consequently, such other poets as Edgar Lee Masters, Orrick Johns, William Carlos Williams, and the unmentioned Carl Sandburg, T. S. Eliot, Wallace Stevens, John Rodker, and other poets of the "Others" group, who are in the main realists, implicitly critical or analytical of life, or at the most neutrally receptive, are somewhat coolly entertained. Of Mr. Masters Mr. Braithwaite remarks, characteristically, that he "de-affinitizes imagination of mystery"; of the poets who contributed to "Others," that they do not deal with life "but with their own little conception of it,"—which, of course, is precisely what all poets do. To Bliss Carman, on the other hand, he ascribes "magic," "natural symbolisms with . . . supernatural meanings. . . ." Clearly, such an attitude reveals in Mr. Braithwaite a very decided intellectual limitation. Must poetry be all marshmallows and tears? Is it to be prohibited from dealing with ideas, or restricted solely to a contemplation of that small part of our lives which is, in a senti-

mental sense, beautiful? Is poetry to be merely
a perfume reserved for our moments of languor?
Mr. Braithwaite might not say "yes" to this question as it stands, but if it were put in a slightly
different form, he would. And in consequence,
try as he will, he cannot be entirely fair to our
contemporary empiricists. Even in his discussion
of such poets as John Gould Fletcher and Miss
Lowell, amiable and even adulatory as (oddly
enough) it sometimes is, one detects a fundamental
perplexity and lack of understanding.

The trouble with this book is, then, at bottom,
that while it has a rather intriguing appearance
of being judicial, it is really, under the mask,
highly idiosyncratic. This might be redeemed if
Mr. Braithwaite, in any part of his work, showed
himself to be an interpreter possessed of subtlety
or persuasiveness. Unfortunately that cannot be
said. Mr. Braithwaite has, to begin with, a
singular incapacity for perceiving the real meanings of words. He uses words in an orotund,
meaningless way; words like "essence," "substance," "mystery," "symbolism," are for ever on
his tongue. For this reason a great part of his
book is thin reading; it is often impossible, except

through the exercise of considerable imagination, to get any meaning out of it whatever. It is possible indeed that his inability to associate words precisely with the ideas for which they stand is the central secret of Mr. Braithwaite's failure as a critic: the cloudy inaccuracy of style may well be simply another aspect of an attitude of mind which has determined his predilection for vaguely interpretative rather than judicial criticism. It may equally account for the extraordinary lack of discrimination which leads him to discuss, not so many kinds of art (which would be merely catholic), but so many qualities of art, as if on one level of excellence. Brilliant, good, mediocre, and downright bad; subtle and commonplace; cerebral and sentimental,—all are treated as of equal importance, and, apparently (as indicated by the last pair of contrasted terms), without any keen awareness of their differences. When he is beyond his depth, Mr. Braithwaite simply takes refuge in words. "Every sense is evocative and intuitional," he says. "Mysticism and wonder are the vital nerves which connect the outer world of reality with the inner world of spirit. Does it matter how the substance is shaped, so long as it is given a being?" This is mere word-blowing; and Mr. Braithwaite's book is full of syllogisms equally ghostly.

Shall we never learn that there is nothing mysterious or supernatural about poetry; that it is a natural, organic product, with discoverable functions, clearly open to analysis? It would be a pity if our critics and poets were to leave this to the scientists instead of doing it themselves.

XI

Romantic Traditionalism: Alan Seeger

IF Freud's theory of the artist is correct—that the artist is one in whom the pleasure principle of childhood never gives way to the reality principle of maturity—then we have a particularly typical artist, in this sense, in Alan Seeger. Alan Seeger was one of that large class who never see the world as it is, who always see it as they wish it to be. To a considerable extent that is true of all of us. We all remain children at least in part. The difference between the normal human being (if there is any) and the artist is merely quantitative; the artist, in addition to his power of speech, keeps more of the child's instinct for living in the imagination, for avoiding contact with the somewhat harsh—or, at any rate, indifferent—world of reality. There is, of course, another type of artist—the type to which Shake-

speare, Euripides, Balzac, Turgenev and Meredith belong—which develops the pleasure principle and reality principle side by side, achieving
the perfect balance which we call greatness.
That type is rare and for the present does not
concern us.

Alan Seeger belongs conspicuously to the
former class. He was sensitive, retiring, idiosyncratic, lived very much if not exclusively in books
during his youth, and developed the art of self-
delusion to an extraordinary pitch. He cut himself off almost entirely from the real world of
real (and, from his viewpoint, somewhat uninteresting) men and women, and equally so from any
intellectual contact with it. An aesthetic attitude
was all he believed in assuming toward the world
which he was capable of perceiving, and in consequence he devoted his energies to the perfecting of
himself as a sensorium. Thought, no doubt,
seemed to him a thing essentially painful and to
be avoided. The result of this characteristic in
his poetry is precisely what we should expect. It
is somewhat archaically romantic; mellifluous, always, in the effort to be sensuously decorative; a
little self-consciously poetic. It is the kind of
poetry which begins by omitting all words which

seem to belong to prose; it divides speech into two
classes, poetic and prosaic, and selects for its
artificial purpose only the lovely (when taste is at
its best) or the merely sensuous or pretty (when
taste subsides a little). One gets, therefore, in
reading Seeger's poems a mild and never intense
pleasure. Vague sights and sounds, vague because
somewhat cloudily seen and heard by the poet,
flow past in pleasant rhythms. Nothing disturbs.
All is as liquid and persuasive as drifting in a
gondola. There are no ideas to take hold of, no
emotions so intense as to shake one's repose. One
has a drowsy impression of trees, flowers, ponds,
clouds, blue sky, old walls, lutes; and youth in the
foreground engaged in a faintly melancholy
anguish of love. The tone of these poems,
whether in the fragmentary and static narratives,
or in the measured sonnets, seldom varies.

In short, Alan Seeger was a belated romantic
poet—and a romantic poet without any peculiar
originality. He had a keen ear, a flexible
technique—but nothing new to say, and no new
way of saying what had been said before. His
verse, throughout, is a verse of close approximations; it is always mother-of-pearl, but seldom
pearl.

XII

A Pointless Pointillist: Ezra Pound

IF one might conceive, in the heliotrope future, any Ph. Demon so inspired as to set about compiling a list of dull books by interesting authors, one could hardly doubt that Ezra Pound's "Pavannes and Divisions" would be his first entry. An incredible performance! Somehow, one has had all these years (for alas, Mr. Pound's indiscretions can no longer be called the indiscretions of youth) the impression that this King-Maker among poets was quite the most mercurial of our performers. One associated with his name the deftest of jugglery, sleights of mind without number, lightning-like tergiversatility, and a genius for finding the latest procession and leading it attired in the most dazzling of colours. Of course, Mr. Pound has himself been at some pains to encourage us in this view. As a publicist he has few equals. But surely it has not been entirely a deception! . . . And nevertheless he comes now upon us with "Pavannes and Divisions"—"a collection," says Mr. Knopf, "of the best prose written by Mr. Pound during the last six years"—and therewith threatens, if we are not careful, to destroy our illusions about him for ever.

For, regrettable as is the confession, the outstanding feature of this book of prose is its dulness. One reads more and more slowly, encountering always heavier obstacles, and—short of a major effort of the will (and a kind of amazed curiosity)—one finally stops. Intrinsically therefore one may say at once that the book is without value. If one is to examine it carefully, one does so for quite another reason; namely, because Mr. Pound is himself an interesting figure—(observe his portrait in this volume, so elaborately and theatrically posed)—a curious representative of *homo sapiens*, and without any doubt a poet who has (sometimes severely) influenced his fellow poets. "Pavannes and Divisions" shall be to us therefore what the soliloquies of the patient are to the psychoanalyst.

If we pass over the unoriginal parts of this book —the clever translation of Laforgue, and the well-

selected dialogues of Fontanelle, amusing but nugatory—and if we listen with concentrated attention to the Mr. Pound who chatters to us, alternately, in the lumberingly metrical and crudely
satirical doggerel of "L'Homme Moyen Sensuel,"
or the disjointed and aimless prose of the essays
and fables, what emerges from this babble? A
portrait, sharp-featured as Mr. Pound's frontis-
piece, but how infinitely more complex—a portrait
which surely not even a Vorticist could compass.
One is reminded, indeed, of Mr. Sludge, so inex-
tricably the most sterling platitudes and the most
brazen quackeries (no doubt believed in) are here
commingled. Add to this that Mr. Pound, like a
jack-in-the-box, takes a naïve delight in booing at
the stately; that he has the acquisitive instincts of
the jackdaw (with a passion for bright and shining objects, particularly those spied from a very
great distance); that he is unhappy unless he can
be rebelling at something or somebody (even at
himself of the day before yesterday—and this is
healthy); and finally that as a poet he has genius,
and has given us more than a handful of beautiful
lyrics—and one begins to perceive that Mr.
Pound's middle name should have been not
Loomis but Proteus. Those to whom Mr. Pound

is a thorn in the flesh will say that it is amazing that the poet of "Cathay" should, in "Pavannes and Divisions," reveal himself so hopelessly as of third-rate mentality : those who are charitable will say that if a poet is to live he must also be a journalist. There is no chance for an argument, since one cannot possibly tell how seriously "Pavannes and Divisions" is intended. But if one cannot read Mr. Pound's intentions, his accomplishment is obvious and disillusioning. If a poet must be a journalist, let him be a good one! And this Mr. Pound is not.

For in point of style, or manner, or whatever, it is difficult to imagine anything much worse than the prose of Mr. Pound. It is ugliness and awkwardness incarnate. Did he always write so badly? One recollects better moments in his history and one even now finds him, as in the first paragraph of his paper on Dolmetsch, making a music of prose. For the secret of this decay one must turn, as in all such cases, to the nature of the man's mind, since style is not a mere application or varnish but the unconscious expression of a nature. And here is encountered one of Mr. Pound's chief characteristics, one that has from the very beginning been steadily growing upon him and—it might be added—steadily strangling his creative instinct. This characteristic is his passion for the *decisive*. His strokes are all of an equal weight and finality. On the sensory plane this first manifested itself, no doubt, as a desire for the single and brilliant image. In logic or dialectics it became a passion for the point, glittering and deadly. In the field of aesthetics it has revealed itself as a need for espousing the out-of-the-way and remote and exceptional, so as to add a sort of impact and emphasis to personality by a solitariness of opinion: it is more striking to play a tune on the Chinese p'i-pa than on the banjo. On these several planes this instinctive appetite has become more and more voracious, more and more exclusive, until finally it has reached a point where it threatens to leave Mr. Pound little else. His poetry has become imageless through excess of image—image too deliberately sought. His prose has become pointless and merely fatiguing because of his effort to point every sentence: it has become a sort of *chevaux de frise*, impossible to walk through. These are failures which, one would think, the artist in Mr. Pound would have foreseen. In prose it is a failure made all the more complete by the fact that the pointillist style was the last style for which he was intellectually fitted. Without the patience for careful analysis, or the acumen and precision and breadth for scientific investigation, this method makes of him merely a subjectivist pedant, a tinkling sciolist, and—what is more amazing for the man who wrote "Cathay"—an apostle of the jejune and sterile. For so intent has Mr. Pound become on this making of points and cutting of images that he has gradually crystallized from them a cold and hard doctrine, a doctrine of negative virtues, aimed primarily against aesthetic excess, but in the upshot totally inimical to that spontaneity and opulence without which art is still-born. In short, Mr. Pound has become, as regards style, a purist of the most deadly sort. So absorbed has he become in the minutiae of aesthetics, so fetichistic in his adoration of literary *nugae*, that he has gradually come to think of style and filigree as if the terms were synonymous. This is the more lamentable because his aesthetics, as revealed in his prose, are by no means subtle. One cannot rear a palace of filigree: nor can one compose a Hamlet or a Tyl Eulenspiegel entirely of velleities and evanescent nuances. Young authors, let us grant with Mr. Pound, must learn to be artisans before they can complete themselves as artists. But at the point where purism stifles exuberance and richness (the intense confession of the sub-conscious) and at the point where, as an aesthetic measure, it prefers the neatly made to the well-felt or the profoundly thought, it becomes obviously vicious.

It is the critic's license to over-refine his point for the sake of emphasis, and this perhaps, in the present case, we have clearly done. To restore the balance somewhat we should add that, though by no means profound, Mr. Pound is provocative and suggestive in his essays on the troubadours and the Elizabethan translators, and refreshing in his papers on Dolmetsch and Remy de Gourmont. After all, is he perhaps, in his prose, deliberately a journalist? . . . And we remember with gratitude that he is a poet.

XIII

Poetic Realism: Carl Sandburg

IT is one of the anomalies of the present poetic revival in this country that it is not dominated by any one single group or tendency, but shared in and fought for by many: classicists, romanticists, and realists, of varying degrees of radicalism, all exist simultaneously, so that we have a spectacle to which perhaps no era was ever before treated,—a complete cycle of poetic evolution presented not in the usual span of two centuries, more or less, but in the space of two years. Those who are interested in poetry are today permitted to watch a three-ringed circus, and to distribute their applause as they please; with a fair certainty that they will find something worth applauding. The rivalry is keen. Nobody will hazard a guess as to which ring will dominate the circus. But so long as the competitors are goaded on by the feats of their rivals to new and more astonishing acrobatics, it does not so much matter.

SCEPTICISMS

More akin to Mr. Masters, perhaps, than to
Mr. Frost, Carl Sandburg nevertheless has character of his own,—whatever we think of his work
we cannot deny that it is individual, that it has
the raciness of originality. The cumulative effect
is one of vigour, a certain harshness bordering on
the sadistic, a pleasant quality of sensuousness in
unexpected places, ethical irony,—and sentimentality. Mr. Sandburg is a socialist, and consistently preaches socialist morals. Next to his de-
ficiencies as regards form, it is perhaps Mr. Sandburg's greatest fault that he allows the poet to be
out-talked by the sociologist. If Tennyson is now
regarded as a tiresome moral sentimentalist, who
knows whether a future generation, to whom many
of Mr. Sandburg's dreams may have become realities, will not so regard Mr. Sandburg? That is
the danger, always, of being doctrinaire. Doctrine is interesting only when new.

Mr. Sandburg restricts himself almost entirely
to free verse: among free verse writers he is the
realist, as the Imagists are the romanticists. But
the free verse of the Imagists is a highly complex
and formal vehicle by comparison with Mr. Sandburg's free verse: it is comparatively seldom that
Mr. Sandburg betrays anything more than a rather

rudimentary sense of balance or echo. For the most part, he employs a colloquial, colourful journalese prose, arranged either in successsions of sharply periodic sentences, each sentence composing one verse-line, or in very long and often clumsy sentences formed of successive suspended clauses, a suspense which he ultimately relieves by a return to the periodic. In other words, Mr. Sandburg is so intent on saying, without hindrance whatsoever, precisely what he has it in his mind to say, that he will not submit to the restraints of any intricate verse-form, even of his own invention, but spreads out in a sort of gnomic prose. There are exceptions, of course: in such poems as "Sketch," "Lost," "Fog," "White Shoulders," "Graves," "Monotone," "Follies," "Nocturne in a Deserted Brickyard," "Poppies,"—and there are others, too,—there is movement, balance, sometimes a return by repetition, sometimes a return by echo. But even in these the movement, balance and return are often those of a rhetorical and orotund prose rather than of verse. The rhythm is slurred, unaccented, in fact a prose rhythm, with interspersions of single lines or groups of lines which rise to a simple cantabile sometimes a little astonishing in the context. These are Mr. Sandburg's lyric moments—the moments when the sentimental Sandburg masters the ethical or ironic Sandburg. Some of the poems listed above, and others, such as "Pals," "Gone" (which has a delightful balance), "Used Up," "Margaret," are almost completely rhythmic, rhythmic in a simple and unsubtle sense, with a regular and easily followed ictus. These are short flights, they suggest, —as indeed all of Mr. Sandburg's work suggests, —the penguin aeroplanes in which novice aviators are trained: at the maximum speed the penguin barely manages to lift from the ground, and to achieve a sort of skipping glide.

Now, if these observations on Mr. Sandburg's technique are in any measure accurate, it becomes important to know whether for his sacrifice of form Mr. Sandburg receives sufficient compensation from the increased freedom of speech thus obtained. Has Mr. Sandburg by sacrifice of those qualities of verse which appeal to the ear, and in some measure to the eye, been enabled to say anything which could not have been said more beautifully, or more forcefully, by a keener use of symmetry? For the present critic the answer must, on the whole, be negative. In a general sense, Mr. Sandburg's material is the material of Frost,

CARL SANDBURG

Masters, Gibson, Masefield: the dominant characteristic of all five men is the search for colour and pathos in the lives of the commonplace. Mr. Sandburg is less selective, that is all,—he spills in the chaff with the wheat. With much that is clear, hard, colourful, suggestive, there is much also that is muddy, extraneous, and dull. The other members of the realist school use the same material, but, being defter artists, use it better. What Mr. Sandburg adds is the sociological element, which is the least valuable part of his book. Ethics and art cannot be married.

In this, I think, we get at the whole secret of Mr. Sandburg's weakness: he does not completely synthesize, or crystallize his poems. He always gives too much, goes too far. His poetic conception is not sufficiently sharp, and in consequence his speech cannot always be sufficiently symmetrical or intense to be called poetic speech. Clear thought brings clear expression, and the converse also is true, as Croce says. Something of the sort is true of the writing of poetry. The clearer, the more intense the emotion or idea, the more direct, forceful, beautiful, and rhythmic will be the expression of it. By a graded scale one passes from the more to the less intense, and that is the passage from poetry to prose. Examine carefully even the more rhythmic of Mr. Sandburg's poems, and you will almost invariably find, even in poems of four lines or less, that the poem can be improved by the omission of one or more lines, one or more ideas, which only cloud the mood. It is no use arguing that Mr. Sandburg deliberately adopts this cumulative and arhythmic method, as Whitman did, out of genuine belief that such a method is truer, or subtler, than any other. The fact is that in such cases the temperament comes first, the theory afterwards: we write in such and such a way because it is the only way in which we can write. If we can then persuade others that our way is best, so much the better—for us.

Classification is apt to seem more important than it really is. It has been many times said during the past few years that it does not so much matter whether a work be called poetry or prose, provided it be true, or beautiful. This study might be closed, then, by simply asking a question: is Mr. Sandburg a realistic poet, or a poetic realist? It is of no importance that the question be answered. It is only important, perhaps, that it shall have been asked.

XIV

A Note on the Evolution of a Poet: John Masefield

THE hasty critic who, when "Good Friday" was published, lamented that book as final proof of the decline of Mr. Masefield, meets something of a poser in "Lollingdon Downs." Mr. Masefield is of that type of creative artist which is most distressing to the critic with a mania for classifying: he will not remain classified; he is for ever in a process of evolution. This is indeed the highest compliment that could be paid him. It is not every poet who is capable of growth and change of a creative sort. With most poets the only marked modifications from book to book are technical. They adumbrate in one book what they achieve in the next. They mark out their province, they develop it, they exploit it, and at last they exhaust it. Consistency, emotional as well as intellectual, rides them as heavily

as the Old Man of the Sea. They are the one-
strain poets, of whom we become accustomed to
expect always the same sort of tune. From a psychological viewpoint this is significant. It means
that these poets have early in their poetic career
achieved what is for them a satisfactory abstrac-
tion, or algebra, of experience. They have
formed crystalline convictions which will hence-
forth be hard, clear, and insoluble. In so far as
we value their viewpoint, or have experienced it,
we enjoy their work and give it a place in the
gamut of our perceptions. But they have ceased
to interest us as individuals, because they inform
us obliquely that for them the problems have all
been solved and there is no longer any flux in
values.

More interesting, therefore, is the poet who, if
he does not always progress intellectually (a hard
thing to determine on any absolute grounds), at
any rate changes; he provides us with a personal
drama as well as a literary. Mr. Masefield is of
this sort. If we look back on his career as poet,
we see a perspective of ceaseless change. His first
mood, in "Songs and Ballads," was unreflectingly,
colourfully lyric: he was preoccupied with sensuous beauty, and with its transience, in the roman-

tic tradition. In the group of novels which followed, we see a steady shifting of the attention
away from the merely romantic, or decorative, and
toward the real and human. The romantic attitude is not eliminated, to be sure; one feels here as
later in the four long narrative poems which gave
Mr. Masefield his greatest success, that though the
material is often rudely naturalistic, it is still being used to an essentially romantic end. It is the
romance of the realistic, of the crude and violent;
it is romantic because it is always seen against a
background of permanence and beauty. This use
of the realistic element, the vigour of the commonplace, reached its height in "The Everlasting
Mercy," "The Widow in the Bye Street," and
"Dauber." In "The Daffodil Fields," which followed, one perceives the next change,—a distinct
relenting of the naturalistic mood, a softening of
both material and technique nearly to the point of
sentimentalism. The hunger for hardness and
virility having been satisfied in a brief and mag-
nificent debauch, Mr. Masefield returned to his
more natural taste for the sensuous and lyric.
The poetic plays which followed were further developments of this. In spirit they are closely akin
to the three later poetic narratives: the motive

force, the emotional compulsion, is an almost obsessive feeling for the tragic futility of man's endeavour in the face of an outrageous and apparently unreasoning fate. At this everlasting door, Mr. Masefield says in effect, we beat in vain. One perceives in Mr. Masefield, as he says this, an almost pathetic bewilderment that it should be so, —but a bewilderment which has not yet reached the intensity of interrogation or rebellion. This point was finally reached in the sonnet series which composed the greater part of "Good Friday." In these one gets a blind and troubled searching for spiritual comfort, a cry for some sort of assurance that beauty is more than a merely transient and relative thing. The tone at its best is tragic, at its worst querulous. The oracle is dumb, however, and Mr. Masefield implies, though he does not state (and in spite, too, of his passionate adherence to Beauty), that the silence is negative.

In short Mr. Masefield's evolution as a poet has been cyclic—it has revolved through many changes, but always about one centre. This centre, which has been at times obscured, and of which Mr. Masefield himself, like most poets, has been perhaps partially unconscious up to the present, is essentially romantic: it is clearly in the tradition of that romanticism which consists in a pagan love of beauty, on the one hand, and a profound despair at its impermanence and relativity, on the other. The sonnets in "Good Friday" showed us that Mr. Masefield had become partly aware that this particular emotional well was the feeding spring of his whole nature: it was his first attempt to dip directly from the source. Now, in "Lollingdon Downs," he has completed this process. The echo of personal complaint which hung over the former work is practically eliminated. Mr. Masefield has seen himself in a detached way, as he might see a reflection; the tone has become one of calm and resignation; like Meredith he has managed a certain degree of objectivism and can accord without undue desolation when Meredith exclaims

> Ah what a dusty answer gets the soul
> When hot for certainties in this our life!

This volume has a singular and intriguing unity, a unity broken up by interludes and by a succession of changes in the angle of approach, and in time and place. The effect is that of a several-voiced music. It is panoramic, rich in perspective,—passing all the way from lyric and reflective sonnets to terse poetic dialogues and narrative lyric almost ugly in its bareness. It would be idle to pretend that Mr. Masefield is a philosopher. He is not intellectual except in the sense that he is tortured by an intellectual issue; he is neither subtle nor profound. But he feels this issue intensely, and even more than usual he strikes music and beauty from it. On the technical side he has few superiors in power to write richly, richly not merely from the imaginative point of view, but also from the melodic. He modulates vowels with great skill; he knows how to temper sensuousness with vigour. Best of all, he is preeminently Anglo-Saxon in his speech.

XV

The Higher Vaudeville: Vachel Lindsay

ONE of the most necessary, but certainly the saddest, of the critic's many detestable functions is the writing of epitaphs. It is never pleasant to have to set the seal of death on the brow that inclines for a crown. There is always, moreover, the horrible chance (or is it horrible—for any save the critic?) that the ghost will walk, that the apparently dead will come to life. Nevertheless, this paper must be an epitaph. Vachel Lindsay is marked out for an at least temporary *hic jacet.*

Mr. Lindsay has never been an easy poet to place or appraise. Of his originality there can be no question. Unfortunately, originality is comparatively a small part in the writing of good poetry—it is the seasoning of the dish, but not the dish itself. Mr. Lindsay has always toyed dangerously with theories about the function of poetry, and these theories—particularly those that concern the revival of the troubadour, and the invention of a declamatory and orotund style in poetry especially adapted to that end—have always, like an internal cancer, threatened the vitality of his work. To begin with, he made the serious mistake of assuming (implicitly at least) that in order to interest the common people, to make poetry genuinely democratic, one must be topical. One sees the effect of this in such a poem as "Gen. William Booth Enters Into Heaven." In the present critic's opinion that is one of the most curiously overestimated of contemporary poems, and, by its very topicality (as well as by its too jingling use of rhyme and rhythm) is destined to short life. In the last analysis it is thin and trivial; the particular has not been raised to the plane of the universal. In his "Moon Poems" Mr. Lindsay allowed his talent for delicate fancy free play with far better results. In "The Congo," too, there was rhythmic beauty and barbaric colour—almost enough, at any rate, to compensate for the rather childish echolalia, the boomlay-booms and rattle-rattle-bings; though even here one wonders whether these blemishes are not terrible enough

to preclude the poem from any other immortality
than that of the literary curiosity. In all these
poems, however, as in "The Fireman's Ball," the
"Sante Fé Trail" and "Sleep Softly, Eagle Forgotten," one felt keen pleasure in Mr. Lindsay's
sonorous vowels, broad and rugged rhythms and
lavish colour. One might deny him any very serious estimate, but none the less one admitted his
charm and skill as an entertainer.

In "The Chinese Nightingale," however, any
hopes one might harbour as to Mr. Lindsay's real
potentialities as a poet are for the time lamentably
set at rest. With the partial exception of the title
poem this book is Mr. Lindsay's own *reductio ad
absurdum* of the poetic methods and theories he
has so much at heart. In "The Chinese Nightingale" itself, in spite of many passages of an even
more delicate lyrical beauty and magic than anything in its prototype, "The Congo," one feels
clearly a decay of the metrical and linguistic fibre;
something has gone wrong, the machine is whir-
ring down, one experiences a sensation of looseness
and flatness. What has happened? One turns
with alarm to the other poems in the book and
one's premonitions prove all too true. Here for
the most part is only a tired and spiritless echo

of the rhythms that once were spontaneous. The tricks stand out like the bones of a skeleton— meaningless refrains endlessly reiterated, page after page of insipid lines, platitudinous ideas, banalities, trivialities, boyisms of rhyme and metre. Sometimes Mr. Lindsay seems to be wearily going through the motions that once made a kind of magic; sometimes he seems to be hopelessly attempting his turn at a sort of heartless and bloodless *vers libre*. The result in either case is a dulness seldom relieved . . . often relieved, indeed, only by one's amazement at the author's solemn inclination to ambitions so childish, performances so amateurishly and stalely inept. This is, in fact, topical journalistic verse, in which the lack of gusto or subtlety is only too fiercely emphasized by Mr. Lindsay's addiction to the use of refrains. The poems on "Kerensky," "Pocahontas," "Niagara," "The Tale of the Tiger Tree" all are examples of this. For any trace of Mr. Lindsay's former charm one must turn to the lyric called "The Flower of Mending," or to "King Solomon and the Queen of Sheba." For once, in the latter poem, Mr. Lindsay's eternal mockingbird, his infatuation for refrain, serves him a good turn.

VACHEL LINDSAY

Can one safely prophesy about any poet? It is doubtful. It is taking no very long chance, however, to guess that if Mr. Lindsay's abilities are to produce work which will survive in all its force he must abandon many of his theories, suppress the good natured buffoon, who, in this case, so often takes the place of the poet, and remember that it is the poet's office not merely to entertain, but also, on a higher plane, to delight with beauty and to amaze with understanding.

XVI

New Curiosity Shop and Jean de Bosschère

I

WHO it was that started the current poetic fad for curio-collecting is a question not hard to answer: Ezra Pound is the man, let the Imagists and Others deny it as loudly as they will. Pound has from the outset, both as poet and as critic, been a curio-collector—a lover of trinkets, *bijoux* of phrase, ideographic *objets de vertu*, carved oddities from the pawn-shops of the past, aromatic grave-relics, bizarre importations from the Remote and Strange. There is no denying, either, that it is a delightful vein in verse. No great exertion is demanded of the reader; he is invited merely to pause before the display-window and to glance, if only for a moment, at the many intriguing minutiæ there arranged for him in trays. Is he tired of struggling with the toxic energies of a Rodin?

JEAN DE BOSSCHÈRE

Then let him rest in contemplation of a carved ushabti. Does a Strauss drag his spirit through too violent a progression of emotional projections? Does a Masters overburden him with relevant facts? A Fletcher fatigue him with aesthetic subtleties prolonged? Let him concentrate on a gargoyle.

This method in the writing of poetry is to be seen at its purest in the Others anthologies, the second of which Mr. Alfred Kreymborg has edited, apparently undeterred by the success of the first. Nevertheless it is a variegated band that Mr. Kreymborg has assembled, and if they have in common the one main tenet—that their poetic business is the expression of a sensation or mood as briefly and pungently (and oddly?) as possible, with or without the aids of rhyme, metre, syntax, or punctuation—they are by no means the slaves of a formula and present us with a variety that is amazing. There is much here, of course, that is merely trivial, and a measurable quantity of the proudly absurd and naïvely preposterous; but if there are no such outstandingly good things here as "The Portrait of a Lady" by T. S. Eliot in the earlier issue, or Wallace Stevens's "Peter Quince at the Clavier," or John Rodker's "Marionettes,"

SCEPTICISMS

we can pass lightly over the studiously cerebral obscurantism of Marianne Moore, the tentacular quiverings of Mina Loy, the prattling iterations of Alfred Kreymborg, the delicate but amorphous self-consciousness of Jeanne d'Orge, Helen Hoyt, and Orrick Johns, and pause with admiration and delight before the "Preludes" and "Rhapsody of a Windy Night" by T. S. Eliot, and "Thirteen Ways of Looking at a Blackbird" by Wallace Stevens. It is not that one is at all indifferent to the frequent charm and delicious originality (at least as regards sensibility) of the other poets, but that one finds in the two last mentioned not only this delicate originality of mind but also a clearer sense of symmetry as regards both form and ideas: their poems are more apparently, and more really, works of art. In comparison, most of the other work in this volume looks like happy or unhappy improvisation. It is significant in this connection that Mr. Eliot uses rhyme and metre, a telling demonstration that the use of these ingredients may add power and finish and speed to poetry without in any way dulling the poet's tactile organs or clouding his consciousness—provided he has the requisite skill. Mr. Eliot's "Preludes" and "Rhapsody" are, in a very minor way, masterpieces of black-and-white impressionism. Personality, time, and environment—three attributes of the dramatic—are set sharply before us by means of a rapid and concise report of the seemingly irrelevant and tangential, but really centrally significant, observations of a shadowy protagonist.

II

From Mr. Eliot to M. Jean de Bosschère, the Flemish poet whose volume "The Closed Door" has now been translated into English by Mr. F. S. Flint, is a natural and easy step. It would appear, indeed, that Mr. Eliot has learned much from M. de Bosschère; certainly he is, in English, the closest parallel to him that we have. It is a kind of praise to say that in all likelihood Mr. Eliot's "Love Song of J. Alfred Prufrock" would not have been the remarkable thing it is if it had not been for the work of Jean de Bosschère: in several respects de Bosschère seems like a maturer and more powerful Eliot. What then is the work of M. de Bosschère?

To begin with, and without regard to the matter of classification, it must be emphatically said that this book has the clear, unforced, and capti-

·vating originality of genius. Whether, as Miss Sinclair questions doubtfully in her introduction, we call him mystic or symbolist or decadent—and all these terms have a certain aptness—is after all a secondary matter. These poems, in a colloquial but rich and careful free verse, occasionally using rhyme and a regular ictus, very frequently employing a melodic line which borders on the prosodic, seem at first glance to be half-whimsical and half-cerebral, seem to be in a key which is at once naïf and gaily precious, with overtones or caricature; in reality they are masterpieces of ironic understatement and reveal upon closer scrutiny a series of profound spiritual or mental tragedies. The method of M. de Bosschère might be called symbolism if one were careful not to impute to him any delving into the esoteric; his themes are invariably very simple. One might call him a mystic, also, if one could conceive a negative mysticism of disbelief and disenchantment, a mysticism without vagueness, a mysticism of brilliantly coloured but unsustaining certainties. But perhaps it would be more exact to say that he is merely a poet who happens to be highly developed on the cerebral side, as well as on the tactile, a poet for whom the most terrible and most beautiful realities are in the last analysis ideas, who sees that as in life the most vivid expression of ideas is in action, so in speech the most vivid expression of them is in parables. These poems, therefore, are parables. In "Ulysse Bâtit Son Lit" we do not encounter merely the deliciously and fantastically matter-of-fact comedy, naïf as a fairy story, which appears on the surface; we also hear in the midst of this gay cynicism the muffled crash of a remote disaster, and that disaster arises from the attitude of the animally selfish crowd towards the man of outstanding achievement. He refuses to be one of them, so they kill him. "They roast Ulysses, for he is theirs." Likewise, in "Gridale," we do not witness a merely personal tragedy; the tragedy is universal. We see the crucifixion of the disillusioned questioner by the unthinking idolaters. In "Doutes," under a surface apparently idiosyncratic in its narration of the humorously bitter discoveries and self-discoveries of a child, we have really an autobiography of disillusionment which is cosmic in its applicability.

And yet he still believes,
This burlesque of a man
Who has given himself a universe

SCEPTICISMS

And a god like an immense conflagration
Whose smoke he smells;
And indeed it is perhaps only a bonfire
Made with the green tops of potatoes.

.   .   .

Nevertheless he still believes,
Ax in hand, this burlesque of a man still believes;
He will cut his dream, four-square, in the hearts of
    men. . . .

.   .   .

There is nothing to laugh at, nothing to object to,
We are not animals
Living to feed our seed.
There is something to believe.
All men are not made of pig's flesh.
There is something to believe.

.   .   .

Who said that I am a poor wretch,
Mere flotsam
Separated from its imaginary god?

Again, in "Homer Marsh," we make the acquaintance of the gentle recluse who loves and is loved
by his house, his fire, his kettle, his pipe and to-
bacco, his dog, his bees; but he goes away to travel,
and lends his house to his friend Peter; and on his
return finds to his bewilderment and despair that
all these beloved things have curiously turned
their affections to Peter.   The tone is lyric, seduc-

tively playful and simple; the overtone is tragic.
It is a translation into action of the profound fact
that ideas, no matter how personal, cannot be
property; that they are as precious and peculiar
and inevitable in one case as in another, a natural
action of forces universally at work.

It would be rash, however, to carry too far this
notion of parables. Some of the poems in "The
Closed Door" are so sensitively subjective, so essentially lyrical, so naturally mystic—in the
sense that they make a clear melody of the
sadness of the finite in the presence of the in-
finite, of the conscious in the presence of the
unconscious—that one shrinks from dropping
such a chain upon them. All one can say is that
they are beautiful, that for all their cool and precise and colloquial preciosity, their sophisticated
primitivism, they conceal an emotional power that
is frightful, not to say heartrending. What is
the secret of this amazing magic? It is not verbal
merely, nor rhythmic; for it remains in translation.
It springs from the ideas themselves: it is a playing of ideas against one another like notes in a
harmony, ideas presented always visually, cool
images in a kind of solitude. It is not that M.
de Bosschère is altogether idiosyncratic in what he

does, that he sees qualities that others do not see; but rather that he combines them unexpectedly, that he felicitously marries the lyrical to the matter-of-fact, the sad to the ironic, the innocent to the secular—the tender to the outrageous. He sees that truth is more complex and less sustaining than it is supposed to be, and he finds new images for it, images with the dew still on them. If novelty sometimes contributes to the freshness of the effect, it is by no means novelty alone: these novelties have meanings, unlike many of those factitiously achieved by some members of the Others group. This is a poet whose quaintness and whim and fantasy are always thought-wrinkled: they are hints of a world which the poet has found to be overwhelming in its complexity. Song is broken in upon by a doubting voice; flowers conceal a pit; pleasure serves a perhaps vile purpose; beauty may not be a delusion, but is it a snare? And what do thought and memory lead to? . . .

Nevertheless he still believes,
Ax in hand, this burlesque of a man still believes. . . .

Ax in hand! It is precisely such bizarre but significant imaginings that constitute the charm of this poet. And it is a part of his genius that, although hyperaesthetic, he is able to keep clearly in mind the objective value of such images, and to contrast them deliciously with the sentimental, or the decorative, or the impassioned.

XVII

Narrative Poetry and the Vestigial Lyric: John Masefield, Robert Nichols, Frederic Manning

IDEAS are like germs: their dissemination is rapid and uncontrollable, and to stamp them out is always difficult, sometimes almost impossible. Moreover their vigour is frequently out of all proportion to their value. Popularity may not necessarily brand an idea as worthless, but there is some reason for regarding such an idea with suspicion. It is fruitful to examine in this light the long since tacitly accepted or implied idea that narrative poetry has outlived its usefulness and that the lyric method has properly superseded it. Since the time of Chaucer and the Elizabethans there has been, needless to say, a good deal of narrative poetry—one thinks of Keats, Byron,

Shelley, Browning, and Morris—but nevertheless in the long interval between the middle of the seventeenth century and the present it is fairly obvious that the focus of popular regard has shifted steadily away from narrative verse and toward the lyric. Is mental laziness the cause of this? One is told that it is too much trouble to read a long poem. It is presumably for this reason that Keats, Shelley, Byron, and Browning are popularly far more widely known for their lyrics than for their more important work. As concerns the relative merits of the two forms the argument is not conclusive.

The lyric began its career, perhaps, as a lyric movement, or interlude, in a longer work. Under the impression, partly correct, that the lyric was, after all, the quintessence of the affair, it was then isolated and made to stand alone. Up to a certain point its justification was its completeness and perfection as an expression of emotion at a moment of intensity. But as a substitute for all that goes to the creation of narrative poetry its test is severer, for if it is entirely to supersede the narrative or dramatic poem it must usurp, and adequately, the functions of that form. And in this regard it may pertinently be asked whether since the days of the Elizabethans the lyric has developed very far.

In fact it would be no very grave exaggeration to say that the lyric method as we have it today is in all fundamental respects of practice the same that we have had since the beginning. The conception of what it is that constitutes the lyric scope has, if anything, petrified. This is particularly true of the nineteenth century, when despite a rather remarkable development of lyric poetry on its technical side—all the way from Keats to Swinburne—the conception of the lyric as a medium for interpretation did not so much broaden as narrow. Did Swinburne really add anything (not, it is meant, to English poetry—to that of course he did richly add—but to poetic method) beyond a perfection of rhetorical impetus, a sensuous timbre of voice? Did Tennyson do more than reset the poetic material of the past to a more skilful, if somewhat too lulling, accompaniment of sound? . . . For any pioneering in the nineteenth century one must turn to Poe, Whitman, Browning, James Thomson ("B. V."), Meredith; and of these the influence has been small, particularly in America, and when felt, felt unintelligently. The popular demand has been great, as always, for the simplest form of subjective lyric, for the I-love-you, I-am-happy, I-am-sad, I-am-astonished-at-a-rose type of lyric, prettily patterned and naïve with a sweet sententiousness. And the supply has been, and still is, all too lamentably adequate to the demand.

It is in reaction to this situation that we largely owe the recent renewal of energy in poetry, signalized in England by the appearance of Mr. Masefield's and Mr. Gibson's poetic narratives, and by the work of the Georgian poets; in America, by the issuance of "North of Boston," "Spoon River Anthology," and the anthologies of the Others and Imagist groups. Two sorts of work are here represented; the dichotomy is obvious, but the initial impulse, the discontent with a lyric method which had become practically vestigial, is the same. Messrs. Frost, Gibson, Masefield, and Masters seek renewal in the broad and rich expanses of realistic and psychological narrative: the lyric poets have sought to refine on sensory perception and delicacy of form. The work of such poets as Mr. Lascelles Abercrombie and Miss Amy Lowell falls between and partakes of the characteristics of both.

Three recent books by English poets illustrate our point: "Rosas," by John Masefield, "Ardours

and Endurances," by R. Nichols, and "Eidola,"
by Frederic Manning. Mr. Masefield's new narrative poem, "Rosas," is a disappointing performance, quite the poorest of his narratives. Mr.
Masefield has always been dubiously skilful at
portraiture; and Rosas, a South American outlaw
who becomes a cruel dictator, seems hardly to have
aroused in his chronicler that minimum of dramatic sympathy without which a portrait is life-
less and unreal. Is Mr. Masefield on the border-
line between manner and mannerism? It is a
danger for him to guard against. His rhetorical
tricks are here, his tricks of sentiment too—not so
overworked as in "The Daffodil Fields" to be sure;
but if "Rosas" avoids the downright pathos of
the murder scene in "The Daffodil Fields," it also
fails to manifest even fragmentarily the psychological intensity and sensory richness of that poem.
The verse is fluent but colourless; the narrative is
episodic, bare, and ill unified. In short, we read
the poem with very little conviction. Most artists make sometimes the mistake of choosing
themes unsuited to them, and it look as if "Rosas"
were the result of such an error. One merely re-
cords one's gratitude that Mr. Masefield has not
yet abandoned narrative poetry.

MASEFIELD AND NICHOLS

Something of the narrative spirit also infuses the work of Mr. Robert Nichols, although in the main it purports to be lyric. "Ardours and Endurances," indeed, is one of the most remarkable of recent first books of verse—perhaps the most remarkable since "North of Boston." Mr. Nichols is young, and one can hardly prophesy of him. At present his style is a rather intriguing blend of Miltonic and new-Georgian strains. The shorter war poems are vigorous, blunt, and genuine; and the "Faun's Holiday," the longest and finest thing in the book, though it is studiously and enthusiastically in the vein of "L'Allegro," can quite well stand comparison with it. One can think of no poet in a decade or so who has come upon us with so richly prepared a sensibility, who takes such a gusto in sensation, or who writes of it with such brio. At this stage in his development a poet may be said hardly to need a theme: anything is an excuse for writing, and with enthusiasm. Whether Mr. Nichols will develop on the intellectual side and use his instinct for word-magic and sound-magic in the articulation of new tracts of consciousness (and that might be considered a definition of the true poet) remains to be seen.

The third volume, "Eidola," by Frederic Manning, is in free verse, and shows an attempt to change the lyric method, but not so much by addition as by refinement. It cannot be said to be very remarkable. The work suggests that of Mr. Aldington, but is more jejunely precise and very much less vivid. . . .

If one finds, therefore, indications of change in the work of Mr. Masefield, Mr. Nichols, and Mr. Manning, one cannot say that in any of these cases it has yet gone very far. They serve chiefly to bring well before us the question whether we are to have a revival of narrative poetry—perhaps more psychological than Mr. Masefield's—or a new orientation of the lyric. Whether or not narrative poetry is doomed to decay, we must hope for two sorts of development in the lyric. In one direction we should get the sort of thing Mr. Maxwell Bodenheim, Mr. John Gould Fletcher, and Mr. Wallace Stevens tentatively indicate for us, a kind of superficially detached colourism, or what corresponds to absolute music; and in the other direction, we should get a development of the dramatic lyric, the lyric presenting an emotion not singly but in its matrix, beginning with the situation which gives rise to it and concluding with the situation to which it has led. Indications of this method are to be found in the work of Mr. Masters, Mr. Frost, and Mr. Eliot. . . . If the lyric is to compete with narrative poetry, or to supplant it, it must certainly develop in the latter of these two manners. If it is merely to evolve further on its own base—and it is hard to see any excuse for its continuance as a mere bonbon for the lazy-mindedly sentimental—it must choose the former.

XVIII

Confectionery and Caviar: Edward Bliss Reed, John Cowper Powys, Joyce Kilmer, Theodosia Garrison, William Carlos Williams

IT would be doing no very frightful violence to the truth to say that one could divide most contemporary American verse into two great types—the types indicated by the title of this paper. If one leaves out of account the matter of poetic form, ignoring for the moment the bitter quarrel between vers-librists and metrists, one could justifiably conclude that all our contemporary poets are purveyors either of confectionery or caviar. Two or three exceptions we must make, of course: Amy Lowell, clearly, serves a *mélange;* and Messrs. Frost, Robinson, and Fletcher, and perhaps Mr. Masters, will escape our classification altogether—which is to their credit. But in the main, it can be plausibly argued that the classification holds.

The confectioners, of course, are in the majority. These are the prettifiers, the brighteners of life, the lilting ones. They fill our standard magazines; they are annually herded by Mr. Braithwaite into his anthology; and now, taking advantage of the poetic decuman wave and the delusions of publishers, they are swamping the land with their sweet wares. The conservative press flings garlands at them, the *Literary Digest* quotes them, the Poetry Society of America (alas!) fêtes them. Hourly they grow more numerous, more powerful. The courageous and creative ones, and those who look to poetry for truthfulness and for a consciousness of life always subtler and more individually worked, will soon have to fight for their lives. And how, indeed, shall they be able to fight? There are no giants to be slain—rather, a host of pigmies, and all alike. A poem by one might bear the signature of any. They sing in chorus rather than singly.

A recent group of volumes by Edward Bliss Reed, John Cowper Powys, Joyce Kilmer, and Theodosia Garrison, is an excellent illustration of this. How many critics, not personally acquainted with these four authors, would know the difference if the names had been shuffled? Mr. Powys, perhaps, would protrude—one would be a trifle alarmed at so much *Weltschmerz*, so many Sphinxes and heathen kisses, so much passionate frustration, in Mr. Kilmer, for example; and one might, the case being reversed, start at Mr. Powys's so speedy conversion to Catholicism. But even here the difference is in the symbols rather than in the literary quality. They are both, they are all, blood brothers—sentimentalists, dabblers in the pretty and sweet, rhetoricians of the "thou and thee" school, pale-mouthed clingers to the artificial and archaic. Here are platitudes neatly dressed, invocatory sonnets, the use of italics for emphasis (that last infirmity!), and all the stale literary tricks so relished especially by the female, —the "calls o' love," the "cries i' the wind," homing birds,—in fact, the whole stock-in-trade of the magazine poet. Of Mr. Reed these remarks are partially unjust. Mr. Reed is too well bred to go so far. He restrains his platitudes from any attempt at lilting; his gait, indeed, is pedestrian. But of Mr. Kilmer and Mr. Powys and Mrs. Garrison—particularly Mrs. Garrison—they are all

too true. Here is nothing new, nothing distinc-
tive, the trotting out of the same faint passions,
the same old heartbreaks and love songs, ghostly
distillations of fragrances all too familiar. Is it
possible for individuals to be so little individual?
Have they never experienced anything for themselves? Ideas, emotions, language, rhythms, all
are oddly secondhand.

The trouble with these poets, at bottom, is simply that they are imitative,—and imitative with a
sentimental bias. Recall for a moment the study
of the mechanism of poetic inspiration made by
M. Kostyleff. The conclusions he reached, whatever else their value, were highly suggestive. An
important part in poetic creation, he maintains, is
an automatic discharge of verbal reflexes, along
chains of association, set in motion by a chance
occurrence. The difference between a poet who
merely echoes the ideas and rhythms of the past,
and the poet who creates something new, is simply
that in the former instance this verbo-motor mechanism is not deeply related to the poet's specific
sensibility; in the latter, it is. This distinction
fits the present case admirably. These poets, in
other words, have not experienced sharply for
themselves. They have drawn their stores of

verbo-motor reactions from the books of others, without checking up from personal observation. They colour their lives to a certain extent in accordance with their too early adoption of a speech which is not their own, instead of colouring their speech in the light of their own experience. They give us, therefore, neither clearness nor truth, nor any beauty of a personal kind. They give us instead a tame uniformity, floods of tepid rhetoric, vague regurgitations of the words of others, varied now and then for good measure with the grotesquely inept and the foolishly naïve. And over and under it all runs our undying American adoration of the pretty-pretty, the pious, the sacred virtues. Life is made out to be simply one sweet thing after another. These are, in fact, confectioners, and not inspired ones, either.

With the question whether there might not arise a great confectioner—one who would bring genius and originality to his task of enlightenment and cheer or, if not that, at any rate another Longfellow—we need not concern ourselves as yet, merely replying that there will be time for discussion when he arises. Meanwhile it is more interesting to turn to a consideration of the type of poetry we have called caviar, and to Mr. William Carlos

Williams, who brings us samples. If the purveyors of confectionery are almost totally lacking in individuality, the purveyors of caviar fly to the other extreme: they carry individuality to excess. These are our modern individualists. What do they care how peculiar or esoteric their idiom is? Self-expression is the thing. If the crowd cannot understand them, or ignores them, so much the worse for the crowd. This is a sentimental attitude, there is a good deal of pose in it, and a consequent defeat is easily regarded by the poet as the martyrdom of the truly great. Nevertheless, it is oddly significant that these caviarists, these purveyors of bitter realism, collectors of the bizarrely unpleasant and the irrelevantly true, have a style entirely their own. M. Kostyleff would admit that their mechanisms of verbo-motor reaction are closely related to their specific sensibilities: they are as clearly original as our other poets are imitative. It seems to be true, in this connection that the realists have a much less stereotyped style than the lilters. They appear to remember that, after all, literature should be drawn from life, not from literature. They experience first (and whole-heartedly, not with a fountain-pen behind the ear) and write afterward.

SCEPTICISMS

Mr. Williams is a case in point. His book throughout has the savoury quality of originality. Is it poetry? That is the question. Self-portraiture it is—vivid, acridly sensuous, gnarled, by turns delicate and coarse. There is humour in it, too, which is rare enough in contemporary verse. But on the whole it is more amiable than beautiful, more entertaining than successful. The reasons for this are several. To begin with, Mr. Williams too seldom goes below the surface. He restricts his observations almost entirely to the sensory plane. His moods, so to speak, are nearly always the moods of the eye, the ear, and the nostril. We get the impression from these poems that his world is a world of plane surfaces, bizarrely coloured, and cunningly arranged so as to give an effect of depth and solidity; but we do not get depth itself. When occasionally this is not true, when Mr. Williams takes the plunge into the profounder stream of consciousness, he appears always to pick out the shallows, and to plunge gingerly. The sensory element is kept in the foreground, the tone remains whimsically colloquial, and as a result the total effect—even when the material is inherently emotional—is still quaintly cerebral. Is it at bottom a sort of puritanism that keeps Mr. Williams from letting go? There is abundant evidence here that his personality is a rich one; but his inhibitions keep him for ever dodging his own spotlight. He is ashamed to be caught crying, or exulting, or adoring. On the technical side this puritanism manifests itself in a resolute suppression of beauty. Beauty of sound he denies himself, beauty of prosodic arrangement too; the cadences are prose cadences, the line-lengths are more or less arbitrary, and only seldom, in a short-winded manner, are they effective. In brief, Mr. Williams is a realistic imagist: he has the air of floating through experience as a sensorium and nothing more. He denies us his emotional reactions to the things he sees, even to the extent of excluding intensity of personal tone from his etchings; and his readers, therefore, have no emotional reactions, either. They see, but do not feel. Is Mr. Williams never anything but amused or brightly interested? The attitude has its limits, no matter how fertile its basis of observation.

Of course, one prefers, in the last analysis, Mr. Williams and his caviar to any amount of thin saccharine. It is at least real. But one concludes that the richer and more vital realm lies

SCEPTICISMS

midway between the extremes: in the truth-tell-
ings of those who not only see sharply and know
themselves intimately, but also feel profoundly,
relate themselves to their world, and tell us what
they know in the comprehensive balanced harmony
which we call art.

XIX

The Return of Romanticism: Walter de la Mare, John Gould Fletcher, William Rose Benét

REALISTIC and romantic movements are commonly supposed, in the cycle of literary evolution, to be alternative. As soon as the one begins to dim, the other begins to glow. But one of the curiosities of the present revival of poetry here and in England has been the simultaneity of these supposedly antipathetic strains. "Sword Blades and Poppy Seed" had scarcely begun to make itself known when the "Spoon River Anthology" and "North of Boston" interrupted the festivities; the first Imagist anthology shrilly intervened only to be rudely jostled by the first Others anthology; and so, ever since, the battle between the realists and the romanticists has been, if unconsciously, at any rate acutely waged, and seems at the present moment no nearer a decision. The explanation of this is not difficult. Reaction is usually the propulsive force of an artistic movement, and in the present case it is possible to maintain that the rebirths of romanticism and realism—a curious pair of twins—were occasioned by a reaction to one and the same situation. This situation was the amazing decrepitude of American poetry, not merely during the last decade or two but, with the exception of Whitman and Poe, during its entire history. In general it may be said that American poetry has been, when romantic, romantic without imagination; when realistic, realistic without intelligence. Of the two strains the former has usually been dominant —a sort of ethical sentimentalism (naïve effort to justify puritanism on aesthetic grounds) supplanting any attempt to think or imagine freely. Home and mother have played the deuce with us.

It is therefore against the failure of the realists to think, and the failure of the romanticists to imagine, that, superficially at least, our modern realists and romanticists have respectively revolted. Are these terms quite adequate? Perhaps not. We might more accurately say that the failure was in both instances a failure of consciousness, a failure to perceive. It is natural therefore that we should now be seeing our realists, on the one hand, constituting themselves psychoanalysts, and our romanticists, on the other, making a kind of laboratory of aesthetics. At the same time, it is a little puzzling to suspect that in a sense the rôles are here reversed. There is something scientific—not to say realistic —in the manner in which our more radical romanticists conduct their researches in aesthetics; and certainly it is an adventurousness bordering on the romantic which impels our more radical realists to the exploration, not seldom, of such sinister, violent, and unfamiliar souls and places. The terms may prove to be outgrown.

If, however, we take refuge in some such statement as that it is the function of romanticism to delight with beauty and the function of realism (psychorealism?) to amaze with understanding, we can have no doubt that Mr. Walter de la Mare's "Motley" and Mr. John Gould Fletcher's "Japanese Prints" are in the romantic tradition. Mr. de la Mare's position as an English poet is as secure as, in a period of such amazing flux, it is possible to have. He could be safely said to share with Mr. William H. Davies first honours as a maker of delightful lyrics. "Motley" his most recent book, will neither add to nor detract from this reputation. It is a little unfortunate that it should have been heralded as signalling an advance and expansion of Mr. de la Mare's talents, for this it clearly cannot be said to do. The most that can be said is that, on the whole, it proves Mr. de la Mare to be still himself—engaging, whimsical, and with a delicious knack for making conventional metres unconventional. One is likely, in appraising the latest book of a poet whose work is familiar, to mistake one's failure to be surprised for a decline or stiffening of the poet's style. It is with some diffidence therefore that one confesses to a feeling that there is not quite the clear magic here that illuminated "Peacock Pie" or "The Listeners," not quite the same joyous plunge, but instead a gray sobriety which does not suit the poet so well. It is still the overtones of the supernatural that Mr. de la Mare plays on most skilfully—and it is these overtones that most definitely impel one to call him a romantic. Here is a search for escape.

It is curious too in the light of Mr. Fletcher's later work (not yet gathered in any book) to find him doing in his "Japanese Prints" precisely this same thing. Recently Mr. Fletcher has been feeling his way towards a kind of realism—an acceptance of (but also an attempt to sublimate) the world of reality. But in "Japanese Prints," even more sharply than in "Irradiations"—and certainly more conventionally than in "Goblins and Pagodas"—we find him participating in the current romantic nostalgia for the remote and strange. As Mr. Aldington and "H. D." have been exploiting Greece, and Mr. Pound and Miss Lowell exploiting China, so now Mr. Fletcher takes his turn with Japan. This whole tendency is indicative of a curious truckling to reason: one desires to talk of beauty and wonder as if they shone at one's very door, but the joyous confidence of youth, the only magician who could make that immanence a reality, has, alas, vanished. Consequently one admits that such things are not to be found at one's humble and matter-of-fact door, and takes refuge in the impalpability and marvel of distance. In "Japanese Prints" Mr. Fletcher has made this excursion neither brilliantly nor badly. These poems are slight, pleasant, sometimes sharply etched, in a few cases magical; but one cannot feel that they will compare very well with "Goblins and Pagodas." Has Mr. Fletcher perhaps a little too studiously attempted the Japanese method of compression and concentration? That is not the style most suited to him: he appears rather to be the sort of poet who reaches his greatest brilliance when allowed to develop rapidly successive musical variations on a theme capable of prolonged treatment. In such work words evoke words, images evoke images, the trains of association function freely and richly; but in work like the present he has restricted himself at the outset to what can be achieved by an effort of intelligence alone, deliberately exerted. It is Fletcher the craftsman imitating Fletcher the poet.

Mr. William Rose Benét's new book, "The Burglar of the Zodiac," proves him certainly to belong with such romanticists, but little else. Mr. Benét is clever, but mechanical. One detects in him a considerable intelligence working through a shallow and unoriginal sensibility. Neither his rhythms nor his color seem to be peculiarly his own, nor has he apparently any sense of effect. His best work is a jargon of approximations.

XX

The Mortality of Magic:
Robert Graves, Roy Helton,
New Paths

MAGIC, whether of diction or of thought, is the one quality in poetry which all poets seek with equal passion. But how different are the wiles of these fantastic huntsmen in pursuit of this golden bird! For some are bold and direct, attempting to slay the creature outright; some go warily with a fine net; some wait in the darkness, hoping to be found rather than to find; while others still—it cannot be doubted—trudge patiently through the forest with a handful of salt. This much their contemporaries may observe of their appearances as huntsmen—but of their success, who can say? For magic is itself a changing thing. The sparrow of today is the phœnix of tomorrow, and vice versa; and tomorrow the captors of sparrows and phœnixes may regard each other with changed eyes.

This, it hardly needs to be said, is largely a matter of diction; and this again is largely a matter of the rate of growth and decay in the language at any given time. Some poets resist the growth of language, some merely acquiesce in it, and some (like Dante and D'Annunzio) exult in and compel it. These last are the boldest spirits, and, on the whole, the most likely to fail. "Will this word live? Will this word die? Will this word, tomorrow, be beautiful or merely vulgar?" In every line they hazard answers to these questions; and the chances are much against any high average of success.

These differences in the attitude towards diction set gulfs between poets who would otherwise be commensals, and constitute the deliciousness and futility of criticism. Observe, for example, the astonishing unlikeness, on this point, of "New Paths," that most interesting English anthology of the verse and prose of the younger men, and the work of two such poets as Robert Graves and Roy Helton. The anthology represents, rather consciously, a band (by no means unvaried) of pioneers—wrestlers with new diction and rhythms, pursuers of new kinds of magic. One could gladly forego, it is true, a sort of Pre-Raphaelitic pinkness and faunishness which crops out here and there, as in the work of the Sitwells. But many of these English huntsmen have attained to a subdued and cool and almost intellectual kind of magic which, in America, we do not know.

At the same time one cannot help feeling a trifle dubious about a charm which is so conscious of itself, so practised in self-exploitation. It is too deliberately naïve, too sophisticatedly primitive. However nicely a poet may write of sirens, fauns, elves, or other superannuated evidences of man's thirst for the supernatural, nowadays it inevitably smacks of affectation.

It is partly because this fault is common in England that one is delighted with such a volume as "Fairies and Fusiliers," of which the American edition has just appeared. This is forthright and honest verse, Anglo-Saxon in its vigorous directness, at the same time irresponsible and sure. Mr. Graves is less ostentatiously serious than his sedater contemporaries in "New Paths," yet one is not certain that in the upshot he does not come off better. Whereas among the younger contemporary poets one finds a good deal of emphasis

on phrase-making for its own sake, here one finds
a poet almost scornful of trappings and colour,
intent only on what he has to say, and saying it
vividly and musically in the unaffected language
of prose. Certainly these are among the most
honest and vivid war poems which so far have
come to us—and if Mr. Graves does not cut very
deep, neither, on the other hand, does he go in for
the usual mock-heroics and sentimental buncombe.
Hear him in "A Dead Boche":

> To you who'd read my Songs of War,
>   And only hear of blood and fame,
> I'll say (you've heard it said before)
>   "War's Hell!" and if you doubt the same
> To-day I found in Mametz Wood
> A certain cure for lust of blood:
>
> Where, propped against a shattered trunk,
>   In a great mess of things unclean,
> Sat a dead Boche; he scowled and stunk
>   With clothes and face a sodden green,
> Big-bellied, spectacled, crop-haired,
> Dribbling black blood from nose and beard.

This approaches, it is true, that sort of romanticism which consists in the deliberate exploitation
of the ugly or horrible. But for the most part

GRAVES AND HELTON

Mr. Graves is a dealer in whim, and it is to Mr. Helton that we must turn to see that method working *in extenso*. "Outcasts in Beulah Land" qualifies Mr. Helton for admission among our realists, but not as yet on a very high level. For the most part his work is still tentative and imitative: one swims successively through currents of Bret Harte, Masefield, Service, and O. Henry. The rhythms are insecure, the narrative psychology undeveloped. Mr. Helton at present finds it difficult to end a story otherwise than in sentimentality or melodrama. At the same time it should be said that these stories are often vivid, richly—if somewhat commonplacely—imagined, and on the whole well-proportioned. Most of one's objections are comprised when one has said that Mr. Helton is young. As for diction, Mr. Helton's method is that of D'Annunzio and Dante: he believes in using the demotic tongue, neologisms and all. He is willing to take his chances that the slang of today will become the magic of tomorrow. Unfortunately he does this without much discrimination; he appears to be somewhat insensitive to values. Even among neologisms it is possible to distinguish vigorous from vulgar, beautiful from merely pretty. And

SCEPTICISMS

it is this which Mr. Helton, like so many of our contemporary pursuers of new magic, has failed to do.

XXI

Varieties of Realism: Wilfrid Wilson Gibson, William Aspenwall Bradley, T. S. Eliot.

MR. WILFRID WILSON GIBSON seems a young man to be giving us his collected poems; it is, in fact, a little startling to find that even if most of his early work is omitted, as in this collection, he has published so much. In addition to the more realistic studies, by which Mr. Gibson has chiefly earned his reputation,—"Daily Bread," "Womenkind," "Fires," "Borderlands and Thoroughfares," "Livelihood," and "Battle,"—this rather unwieldy volume contains also one poem in an earlier vein, "Akra the Slave," a useful reminder that, like his fellow-poet Mr. Masefield, Mr. Gibson has evolved in manner from romanticism to realism. When one considers in this connection some of Mr. Gibson's very latest work, par-

ticularly in the lyric and in the sonnet form,—
where he seems tentatively to be teasing once
more at colours more frankly brilliant,—it is possible to suspect that, again like Mr. Masefield, he
has fed himself to satiety on the drab and realistic
and may yet revert to the romantic, an evolution
altogether natural.

Mr. Gibson's development has, however, been
more obvious and orderly than Mr. Masefield's.
It was not, in his case, a sudden surrender to an
overpowering and perhaps previously unconscious
impulse, but rather a gradual modification. Even
in "Akra the Slave," for example, there are hints
of the close psychological texture which was later
to reach its maximum of efficiency as a poetic
style in "Fires" and "Livelihood." In "Daily
Bread" and "Womenkind," pitched in a colloquial
dramatic form (or dialogue, rather, closely akin
to Mr. Abercrombie's use of the same form in
parts of "Emblems of Love"), there was necessarily a good deal of waste. Mr. Gibson's genius
is not dramatic, and he found himself precluded
from the sort of step-by-step objective analysis
which is his keenest pleasure. Consequently, this
is the weakest part of his work. In "Fires," on
the other hand, lies the happiest synthesis of all

Mr. Gibson's talents. In these brief, rhymed narratives, dealing for the most part with the lives of working-people, but not too insistently in a drab tone, Mr. Gibson found himself free to exploit side by side his love of colour and his love of sharp analysis. The result is a sort of iterative half-lyric analysis, frequently powerful. In "Borderlands," "Livelihood," and "Battle," however, the lyric and colourful aspect has gone dwindling in proportion as the psychological preoccupation has increased. Unfortunately, the gain in truthfulness has not entirely compensated for the loss in beauty. In some of the poems which compose the volume called "Battle," for example, it may be questioned whether actual bathos was not reached: to truthfulness Mr. Gibson seems here to have sacrificed everything, even dignity. One admits his truthfulness, but one does not feel it.

It is, of course, too early to attempt a placing of Mr. Gibson. For the present it is enough to say that he has developed a style peculiarly effective, and valuable too for its influence on contemporary poetry. Mr. Gibson has clearly proved that poetry can deal with the commonplaces of daily life,—with the bitter and trivial and powerful and universal commonplaces of human consciousness,—and do it with force and beauty. None of his contemporaries on either side of the Atlantic has equalled him in power to drag forth, link by link, the image-chain of a human mood. We should not yet begin complaining that these moods have a hypnotic sameness throughout his work; nor that he varies the monotony of these analytical studies with too little of that romantic flush which, one cannot help thinking, no less than an excessive love of matter-of-fact, is a part of consciousness. Mr. Gibson lacks the lyric *élan* for this, just as he also lacks flexibility of technique. But these are questions which perhaps will be settled anew with every epoch according to the prevailing taste; one cannot be dogmatic about them. Today we like Mr. Gibson for his dogged truthfulness, and we shy at his occasional pedestrian sentimentality. A later judge may conceivably reverse the verdict.

Mr. William Aspenwall Bradley is obviously a congener of Mr. Gibson. The poems in his "Old Christmas" are, for the most part, narrative and in much the same form that Mr. Gibson is most fond of using: the octosyllabic couplet. It cannot be pretended that this is poetry of a high order;

GIBSON, BRADLEY, ELIOT

but Mr. Bradley, in adapting to his use the life of the Kentucky mountain-folk, has hit upon extremely interesting material; he has given us some excellent stories, told in the folk-language, with many quaintnesses of idiom, and, on the whole, with the simplicity and economy that makes for effect. Mr. Bradley's technique is useful rather than brilliant—he seldom rises above the level of the story-teller. In "Saul of the Mountains," "Old Christmas," or the "Prince of Peace," the story obviously is the thing, and the story does the trick. When, as occasionally happens, Mr. Bradley shows genuine imaginative power (as in the "Strange Woman" and its sequel) it is hard to say how much that power is fortuitous.

Mr. T. S. Eliot, whose book "Prufrock and Other Observations" is really hardly more than a pamphlet, is also a realist, but of a different sort. Like Mr. Gibson, Mr. Eliot is a psychologist; but his intuitions are keener; his technique subtler. For the two semi-narrative psychological portraits which form the greater and better part of his book, "The Love Song of J. Alfred Prufrock" and "The Portrait of a Lady," one can have little but praise. This is psychological realism, but in a highly subjective or introspective vein; whereas Mr. Gibson, for example, gives us, in the third person, the reactions of an individual to a situation which is largely external (an accident, let us say), Mr. Eliot gives us, in the first person, the reactions of an individual to a situation for which to a large extent his own character is responsible. Such work is more purely autobiographic than the other—the field is narrowed, and the terms are idiosyncratic (sometimes almost blindly so). The dangers of such work are obvious: one must be certain that one's mental character and idiom are sufficiently close to the norm to be comprehensible or significant. In this respect, Mr. Eliot is near the border-line. His temperament is peculiar, it is sometimes, as remarked heretofore, almost bafflingly peculiar, but on the whole it is the average hyperaesthetic one with a good deal of introspective curiosity; it will puzzle many, it will delight a few. Mr. Eliot writes pungently and sharply, with an eye for unexpected and vivid details, and, particularly in the two longer poems and in "The Rhapsody of a Windy Night," he shows himself to be an exceptionally acute technician. Such free rhyme as this, with irregular line lengths, is difficult to write

GIBSON, BRADLEY, ELIOT

well, and Mr. Eliot does it well enough to make
one wonder whether such a form is not what the
adorers of free verse will eventually have to come
to.   In the rest of Mr. Eliot's volume one finds
the piquant and the trivial in about equal proportions.

XXII

American Richness and English Distinction: Ralph Hodgson, Harold Monro, Walter de la Mare

IF there is one respect in which contemporary English poetry is conspicuously and consistently superior to contemporary American poetry, it is in the lyric. While their more adventurous fellowcraftsmen in America have been experimenting, perhaps a little recklessly, with narrative, epic, and symphonic verse, and with bizarre arythmics and insoluble self-symbolisms of all sorts, the English poets, with one or two exceptions, have held more clearly to the lyric tradition. This is not the cause, as some appear to think, for either heartburnings or self-congratulations. Poetry is poetry no matter where or how it is written, art should not be regarded from a narrowly and selfishly national standpoint, and we should be as ready to applaud a foreign artist as an American. As a theory, this is of course a platitude; as a fact, it might in some quarters be regarded as an alarming novelty. As a practice, moreover, it meets opposition because it demands the application of a high degree of fair-mindedness and intelligence. One must face, in all foreign art, a considerable divergence from one's own in temper and method; and face it with understanding. It is different, but is it necessarily inferior?

These problems have been often raised in the last few years over the question as to the relative merits of contemporary English and American poetry. Foolish things have been said on both sides of the Atlantic,—the patriotic instinct has been as vigorous and cloistral in *Poetry and Drama*, of London, as in *Poetry*, of Chicago. In general the failure has been one of understanding, aided in some cases by a disposition to condemn, *a priori*, without consulting the evidence. It is encouraging to see signs that this attitude is breaking down. The fact that the whole poetic firmament is in such a state of chaos has of itself made it necessary for critics to discard easy traditional theories and employ methods a little more empirical. This has resulted in greater fairness to the individual—it has even gone so far, at times, as to indicate complete anarchy, in which bad was as loudly acclaimed as good. The up-shot, however, has been the establishment of a middle attitude of good-humoured, first-hand analysis, toward foreign art as well as domestic.

It is with this attitude that we should approach the work of such poets as Mr. Hodgson, Mr. de la Mare, and Mr. Monro. If we have developed a taste for work more racily American, more conspicuously of the place and moment, we may conceivably feel that we are stepping back two or three decades when we read, for example, the poems of Mr. Hodgson. We should not allow this to prevent our enjoyment of their unique charm and originality. Mr. Hodgson is that rarity in these times, a poet of very small production, and of production on a uniformly high level, a poet who had already earned a reputation before the printing of his first book. His range is not wide. A single tone dominates nearly all the twenty-five poems in his "Poems"— whether in the narrative lyrics, such as "The Bull," "Eve," "The Song of Honour," and "The Gipsy Girl," or in the simple lyrics, such as "Time, You Old Gipsy Man," and "Stupidity

Street." The metrical variety is not great, the melody is always open; but Mr. Hodgson possesses a genuine gift for modulation which carries him safely over inversions that to others would have proved fatal. If Mr. Hodgson's abilities stopped there, his verse would be charming, but empty; these are matters of the voice merely. But Mr. Hodgson's chief value lies rather in what he has to say. There are two arts in poetry: the art of precisely saying what one has in mind; and, even more important (though less regarded), the art of excluding from one's conception all that is not of pure value. It is particularly in this latter respect that Mr. Hodgson excels. His mood is always perfectly clear; the terms by which he states it have a delicate and sweet precision. Seldom is there a waste idea, seldom a waste line. Mr. Hodgson does not, like many poets, have to take a running start, only to generate lyric speed when half way through the poem; neither does he exhaust himself altogether in the first stanza. On the contrary his poems have that clear certainty, from beginning to end, which constitutes excellence in art. This would of course be a dull perfection if it were not for the quality of cool magic which is woven everywhere through Mr. Hodgson's work, varying all the way from the twinkle of whim, as in "Eve," to the graver tones of "The Song of Honour." In general, this magic is not so much the magic of beauty as the magic of unaffected truthfulness,—vigorously phrased, naïve, sincere. One feels little trace of artifice, even in so fluent a lyric as "Eve." And a large part of the effectiveness of "The Bull" is in its honest matter-of-factness.

The most arresting feature of Mr. Hodgson's work, however, is the feature which is most likely to give radical Americans the impression that he is old-fashioned: the fact that though he is essentially a lyric poet (preferring a lyric which is narrative) he is none the less essentially objective, —never, or seldom, speaking in his own voice, or developing, psychologically, any personal or dramatic viewpoint. This is an attitude which predicates poetry as a something separate from our own tortuous lives, a something additional, perfect in itself: a something to turn to for delight, which shall take us, not deeper into ourselves, but away from ourselves. This attitude adds to the charm of Mr. Hodgson's work, but it is also, in a wider sense, a weakness. It means that the greater part of human experience must remain unexpressed by

him. It means that his work, in spite of its
realistic or objective method, is in the last analysis
decorative rather than interpretative. Poetry of
this sort is not a window through which one may
see, but a picture hung on the wall. It aims by
every means known to the art to combine
aesthetic patterns which shall delight us with their
colour and texture; but it never strikes at us
through our emotions. The pleasure it affords us
is serene, cool, detached. Itself produced by no
very intense emotional disturbance in the poet's
brain (beyond the pathos of creation) it has in
consequence no power to disturb the reader. It
does not reach forward or backward in human experience. It is, in fact, all treble, and no bass.
The darker chords of intellectual and emotional
frustration which shake the centre of individuality
itself, and which in the past have given us our
greatest poetry, are here untroubled. In this respect Mr. Hodgson, Mr. de la Mare, and the
Imagists, antipodal as their methods are, all share
essentially one purpose.

The work of Mr. Monro is from this standpoint the direct antithesis of Mr. Hodgson's work.
Mr. Monro is, if the expression may be used, a
psychological realist. If he is by no means the

equal of Mr. Hodgson in point of lyricism or natural magic or roundness of form, he somewhat makes up for this in greater richness and variety and in what must be called, for lack of a better word, the quality of humanness. It is daily, personal experience that interests Mr. Monro— personal experience viewed from the individual centre, observed almost religiously as it flows from moment to moment in the stream of consciousness. This is in the strain which is perhaps the richest in potentialities among modern tendencies in poetry. To a considerable extent it implies the transference of the method of the psychological novel or play to poetry: in the end it is nothing less than a poetic study of consciousness itself. In this respect Mr. Monro's method is right rather than successful. His speech, if robust, is crabbed, muttering, and laborious. His preoccupation with the profound trivialities which make up our lives, though often fresh and delightful, as in parts of the two series called "Week End" and "Strange Meetings," sometimes merely results in amiable catalogues, humourously tinged with panpsychism. Along, too, with a good deal of imaginative richness Mr. Monro displays an unfortunate tendency to push quaintness and whim to the verge of preciosity. Should a train, for instance, be said ever to "tittle tattle a tame tattoon"?—This is an example of a good idea not quite successfully brought to birth. It should be added that Mr. Monro does not do this often, and that, in general, his work has an intellectual saltiness of originality which makes it satisfactory and often delightful reading. And as was said above, it gains in suggestiveness because it is in a strain, as yet infrequent in modern poetry, but probably destined to great importance: the strain of psychological realism; although Mr. Monro cannot be said to have taken that method either far or subtly.

Mr. de la Mare's "Peacock Pie" consists of lyrics ostensibly for children; in reality it contains some of the most delightful work he has done. It is doubtful whether any other living American or English poet can weave simple melody as deftly as Mr. de la Mare, melody both as regards words and ideas. If after a century has passed one may recall Leigh Hunt's categories of imagination and fancy as the two springs of the poetic, it would be no violence to say that Mr. de la Mare's power over us is rather in fancy than in imagination. It is delicate, elusive, impalpable; over the simplest lyrics hangs an overtone of magic. And now and again, as in the "Song of the Mad Prince," this magic reaches a grave intensity which strikes well to the marrow of things. Mr. de la Mare is not an innovator, and his scope is not great; but within his scope he has no superior.

If after a reading of these three rather typical English poets we recall as contrast the dominant notes in contemporary American poetry, certain differences stand out conspicuously. Despite the fact that Mr. Monro manifests a slight orientation in a new direction, we may say that these poets, like most contemporary English poets, hold more or less surely to the main poetic tradition, in particular as concerns the theory that lyric poetry is a decorative rather than an interpretative art, and that its affair should be, primarily, the search for and modulation of beauty, with or without regard to its nearness to human experience. The result is that from a purely literary viewpoint English poetry of the present day is much more perfectly finished, much maturer, than American poetry. On the other hand, it loses proportionately by this very fact. By comparison with contemporary American poetry,—which is more empirical, drawing more boldly on the material of a wider consciousness, without so sharp a literary distinction between the poetic and the non-poetic, and more richly experimental as concerns questions of form, —English poetry appears at once thinner and more "literary." It does not seem to relate so closely to the complete life of the individual. It becomes obvious, in view of this contrast, to hope for some sort of fusion of the two methods. Will the poet arise who will have no occasion for envying either "this man's art" or "that man's scope"? It appears to be only a question of time.

XXIII

Poets as Reporters: Edith Wyatt, Richard Butler Glaenzer, Christopher Morley, A Treasury of War Poetry

POETS, it may be said, quite as clearly as scientists or historians, are reporters for the Journal of Humanity. They are the scientists of the soul, or as others might prefer, of the heart, or of consciousness. We can imagine them sallying forth into the city of consciousness to report to us what is going on there—some of them perhaps to get no further than the main thoroughfare or the shopping centres, while others, bolder spirits, penetrate to obscure and dismal alleys or to suburbs so remote and unfrequented that we are at first inclined to question whether they exist at all. In any generation the great

WYATT, GLAENZER, MORLEY

majority of the ephemeral poets are those who early in life have discovered the park in this city and are for ever after to be found there, loitering. One conceives them as saying: "This is pleasant, so why go farther? No doubt there are mean streets, sinister purlieus, but let us not distress ourselves over them!" If we reproach them for thus misrepresenting our city, for exaggerating the relative importance and beauty of the park, (calling them, as Freud does, wish-thinkers) they can retort that those who ferret out exclusively the mean and sinister are quite as precisely wish-thinkers— impelled, as Nietzsche said of Zola, by the "delight to stink." To this, of course, we reply that our ideal reporter—who turns up only at rare intervals, as a Shakespeare, a Dante, a Balzac, a Turgenev, a Dostoevsky—is the one who sees the city whole. We might also add that those who report extensively on the shabby purlieus are so much in the minority always that they are far more worthy of encouragement than the park loungers. Their influence is, in the aggregate, healthy.

Miss Wyatt, Mr. Glaenzer, and Mr. Morley are all three in this sense devotees of the park. But if they are at one in thus representing the

park as of supreme importance, their reports are
delivered in manners quite distinct.   Miss Wyatt
is clearly more aware than the other two that
there are other aspects to the city—she has
glimpsed them; she alludes to them; she is a little
uneasy about them.   She has heard the factory
whistles at morning and evening, and seen people
going to work.   Is it possible that there is a certain
amount of suffering and fatigue and dulness en-
tailed?   Yes, it is; but at this point she closes
her eyes, and goes into a dactylic trance with regard to wind, rain, flowers, wheat, waterfalls,
sunset over a lake.   Life is beautiful, disturbing;
it moves one to exclamation or subdued wonder.

> The Vesper star that quivers there
> A wonder in the darkening air,
> Still holds me longing for the height
> And splendour of the fall of night.

In these four lines Miss Wyatt gives us her
poetic attitude—hands clasped and lips parted.
A great poet could endow this attitude with dignity and power; but Miss Wyatt is not a great
poet.   She lacks on the one hand the precision,
on the other hand the magic, for the task, though
in such a poem as "An Unknown Country" she

comes close enough to the latter quality to make
us regret that she could not come closer. She
succeeds in making us see how beautiful this poem
might have been, by comparison with which vision
the actual accomplishment leaves us frustrate.
Rhyme and rhythm—particularly the dactyl and
the use of repetition—tyrannize over Miss Wyatt,
frequently to her undoing; and this sort of tyranny
is symptomatic. It relates to a certain emotional
or intellectual incompleteness.

Of the other two poets Mr. Glaenzer is distinctly the more varied. He accepts the park
gladly and without question, and he observes it
carefully. His report is mildly rich, blandly
sensuous, unoriginally tuneful. His observations
are more precise than Miss Wyatt's, his technique
more secure. On the other hand he lacks force
or direction, he seems to be unable to transpose
from one key to another so as to obtain climax,
and the exigencies of rhyme lead him a helpless
captive. It should also be remarked that his sense
of humour occasionally fails him, as when he
directs his plover to exclaim:

Coddle . . . coddle . . . *Hist!*

Expletives of this sort—and one recalls Miss

SCEPTICISMS

Lowell's tong-ti-bumps and Mr. Lindsay's boom-lay-booms—are dangerous, to say the least.

Mr. Morley, one is at first inclined to add, would not have made this error, for one of the dominants in his book, "Songs for a Little House," is humour. And yet, on second thought, that is not so certain, for Mr. Morley has a disheartening talent for spoiling an otherwise refreshingly light or fancifully humorous lyric by collapsing at the close in a treacle of sentimentality. Sentimentality is Mr. Morley's dark angel, and it is curious to see how at the first whisper of its approach his sense of humour either abandons him incontinently or assumes a heavy-footedness and loutishness which suggests the Teutonic—as indeed his sentimentality does also. Thus, as an example of the latter quality:

> Pure as the moonlight, sweet as midnight air,
> Simple as the primrose, brave and just and fair,
> Such is my wife. The more unworthy I
> To kiss the little hand of her by whom I lie.

And of the former:

> More bright than light that money buys,
> More pleasing to discerners,
> The shining lamps of Helen's eyes,
> Those lovely double burners!

WYATT, GLAENZER, MORLEY

One must turn to some of Mr. Morley's sonnets for a maturer and more persuasively imaginative touch, or to his parodies for a surer delicacy of humour. The parodies of Hilaire Belloc and Edgar Lee Masters are excellent.

If these three poets are all determined, as reporters, to emphasize the pretty and sweet and to ignore the surlier and more tragic demons of consciousness, one finds in the anthologies of war verse edited respectively by Mr. W. R. Wheeler and Mr. George Herbert Clark that the disposition to glorify, to escape the unpleasant, is equally prevalent. One would have supposed that by this time war would have become so terribly real as to paralyse any such attempt; yet here they are, hundreds of poets, frantically waving once more the dubious emblems of honour, glory, duty, revenge, self-sacrifice. So unanimous is it that it has almost the air of a conspiracy. An amazing intoxication! Yet truth has many ways of revenging itself, and in this instance it does so by effectively frustrating the effort to beautify war or make pretty poetry of it. For the uniformity or failure in these two collections is nothing short of astonishing. One closes them with the feeling that few if any of these poets,

SCEPTICISMS

even those who have made names for themselves,
have come within a thousand miles of the reality.
They shout, they exhort, they lament, they pæan,
but always with a curious falseness of voice; it is
painfully apparent that they have failed to
imagine, or more exactly, to see. Their verses are
histrionic. For a glimpse of the truth one must
turn to Miss Lowell's "Bombardment," in a richly
imagined and dramatic prose (which Mr. Charlton
M. Lewis dismisses in his preface with patronizing
fatuity), to Rupert Brooke's Sonnets, to Alan
Seeger's "Champagne," or to some of the work of
Mr. Gibson and Mr. de la Mare. For the rest,
one alternates between Kiplingesque narratives of
incident and sterile odes. What is perhaps the
finest poem of the war, Mr. Masefield's "August:
1914," is in neither anthology, nor is Mr.
Fletcher's "Poppies of the Red Year."

Are we to conclude from all this that poetry
cannot be made of war? Not necessarily. What
immediately suggests itself is that as war is hide-
ously and predominantly real, an affair of over-
whelmingly sinister and ugly forces, it can only
be embodied successfully (with exceptions) in an
art which is realistic, or psycho-realistic. To return to the simile with which this review was

WYATT, GLAENZER, MORLEY

opened, we might say that those poets who are devotees of the park rather than of the slum will almost inevitably fail in any attempt to describe war in terms of the park. And to succeed at all is to falsify, to report the desire rather than the fact. It is of such failures—adroitly written and interesting, but ephemeral and with the air of hasty marginal notes—that these two anthologies largely consist. Meanwhile, we await with interest the return of the poets from the trenches. It is possible that we shall then learn what war is: they will perhaps tell us directly and simply and subtly what a human being really thinks and feels in such a fantastic environment. And we shall probably be surprised.

XXIV

Sunt Rerum Lacrimae:
Chinese Poetry

WHEN, a little over a year ago, translations of Chinese poetry began to appear over the signature of Arthur Waley, the literary supplement of the London *Times* devoted a leader to a panegyric of them and, among other things, predicted that the whole course of occidental poetry might well and for that matter might profitably be changed by this spiritual invasion from the East. The writer in the *Times* was most struck by the total absence, in Chinese poetry, of the literary artifices which, for the last twenty-five centuries at any rate, have made occidental poetry what it is. He was moved, as others have been, by the bare simplicity of it, its stalwart and rugged adherence to the homelier facts and truths, its contemplative naïveté, its honesty, and its singularly charming blend of the implicit and the explicit. These are, indeed, the conclusions which nine out of ten readers of Mr. Waley's collection, "One Hundred and Seventy Chinese Poems" might justifiably reach. Mr. Waley has employed as his translation-medium, for the most part, a free verse in which, despite his preface (he appears to consider that he has kept the rhythm of the original), there is hardly a trace of any sort of rhythm other than that of a well-felt prose. But this is a fact which (after a few lines) one has completely forgotten; for Mr. Waley has produced a book which, strictly regarded as a piece of English literature, has a remarkable beauty. As poetry one has little but praise for it. It is a clear enough, and precious enough, addition to our English gamut. If one has any quarrel with it at all, one quarrels with it as a translation.

And here, I believe, there is some ground for thinking Mr. Waley's book misleading. For, as noticed above in the case of the writer in the London *Times*, most people will instantly conclude, after reading these deliciously candid and straightforward free-verse poems, that Chinese poetry is a far simpler and far less artificial affair than ours; and many who already incline towards the less formal of poetic methods will employ this as the final *coup de grace* in their argument against an art of delicate elaboration. Their argument, of course, gains force with the publication of any successful book of free verse; but of the historical argument which Mr. Waley's book seems so completely to afford them they must be deprived. For Chinese poetry is not a poetry even remotely akin to free verse; and it is far from being artless.

As a matter of fact, little as one would gather it from Mr. Waley's preface, or from Judith Gautier's preface to "Chinese Lyrics from the Book of Jade," or from Mr. Cranmer-Byng's preface to "A Lute of Jade"—all of which are in almost equal measure informative and confusing—Chinese poetry is perhaps more elaborately and studiously artificial (as distinguished from artless) than any other. The literary traditions are so powerful and inflexible as to be almost ritualistic. The forms are few and exactly prescribed, the rules many. When it is recalled that the Chinese language is entirely monosyllabic; that the variety of rhymes is small; that all words are, for the purposes of poetry, inflected as either flats or sharps (the inflection for each word being fixed); and that Chinese poetry employs not only rhyme, and an exact number of syllables in each line, but that these syllables must follow a precise pattern in accordance with inflection (equivalent, in a degree, to our ictus), one begins to see how complex an art it is. A typical four-line stanza, for example, with seven words to a line, the cesura falling unalterably after the fourth word, and rhyming perhaps *a*, *a*, *b*, *a*, is as follows:

Flat flat sharp sharp   flat flat sharp
Sharp sharp flat flat   sharp sharp flat
Sharp sharp flat flat   flat sharp sharp
Flat flat sharp sharp   flat flat sharp

Almost all Chinese poetry of the great periods is stanzaic, and almost all of it is short, the quatrain and the poem of eight or twelve lines being the most common lengths. A few poets have essayed longer poems, some of them narrative—notably Po Chü I—but these are exceptions.

It is therefore with all these facts in mind that one should read the translations of Mr. Waley, or Mr. Cranmer-Byng; or Mr. Whitall's translations of the French versions by Judith Gautier. Of the three books, Mr. Waley's is distinctly the most comprehensive and from the literary point of view the most successful. The other two are usefully supplementary however, for the reason that the Cranmer-Byng versions are for the most part metrical and in rhyme, and serve somewhat to correct one's impression that Chinese poetry is non-literary; and that the Whitall book consists largely of love poems, the element in which the other books are weakest. From the three volumes, taken together, emerges the fact that Chinese poetry is among the most beautiful that man has written. Artificial and elaborate it may be as regards the mould into which it is cast; but, at any rate as presented to us in Arthur Waley's book, it seems, by contrast with most occidental poetry, poignantly simple and human. How much of this we must credit to Mr. Waley we cannot, of course, tell. We must remember that it is above all else a poet's *art* which the Chinese set store by. A part of the charm of this poetry, stripped of its art for us who are occidental, must inevitably be simply due to its combination of the strange with the familiar, of the remote with the comprehensible. But one is tempted to go farther and to say that Chinese poetry seems more than any other a cry from the bewildered heart of humanity. Sorrow is the most persistent note in it—sorrow, or sorrowful resignation; sorrow for the inevitable partings of friends, sorrow for the home remembered in exile, for the departure of youth, the futility of a great career, the injustice of man, the loneliness of old age. The Freudians will have something to explain in the remarkable infrequency with which it deals with love between the sexes; it is friendship which is most honored. And perhaps one is wrong in saying that these poems, even as given in the limpid free verse of Mr. Waley, in delicately colloquial prose-rhythms, are altogether artless. The rhythm of ideas is clear; and that sort of dim counterpoint which may be manifest in the thought itself is not less apparent. Simple and homely as appear the details by which these poets evoke a mood, simple and homely and prosaic as the mood itself may appear, it is when one attempts retrospectively to reconstruct the steps by which any such mood-poem was completed that one perceives how exquisitely selective was the poet, with what patient fastidiousness he searched for the clear qualities of things, and with what a magical precision he found just that tone of restraint, almost of matter-of-factness, which fairly whizzed with overtones. A popular form of Chinese poetry is the four-line poem called the stop-short, in which the sense is supposed to continue after the poem has stopped. But even in the longer poems that is almost universally the method. It is the hum of reverberations, after the poem has been read, that is sought for. And even such a narrative poem as Po Chü I's "Everlasting Wrong," one of the famous "long" poems of the language (though it runs only to a few pages), is constructed in accordance with this instinct, and is, therefore, really a sequence of lyrics.

Does all this mean that Chinese poetry is profoundly unlike our own? Perhaps not, in theory. Restraint and understatement have always been characteristic of Anglo-Saxon poetry, though not to the same extent. It is in the sort of theme chosen that one feels the most profound divergence. Our own themes are apt to be sublimated and "literary," to some degree conventionalized, no matter how simple and colloquial may be the treatment. The themes of the Chinese poets are highly conventionalized—the same themes used over and over again—but they are essentially simple. Sunt rerum lacrimae—it is the pathos in things that the Chinese poets play upon, century after century; the inanimate things, the things of humble human use, the small utilities which we associate with lives simply lived, supply the medium through which Li Po or Po Chü I or T'ao Ch'ien pierce our hearts. One is struck by the childlike candour of this poetry: no detail is for-bidden—as it would be in our poetry, perhaps—because it seems too prosaic; the sole question raised is as to its emotional appropriateness. Is it a comb, a fan, a torn dress, a curtain, a bed, an empty rice-bin? It hardly seems to matter. The Chinese poet makes a heart-breaking poetry out of these quite as naturally as Keats did out of the song of a nightingale heard in a spring garden. It is rarely dithyrambic, rarely high-pitched: part of its charm is in its tranquillity, its self-control. And the humblest reads it with as much emotion as the most learned. . . . Was the writer in the London *Times* right, therefore, in thinking that this poetry might be a wholesome influence for our own? If it can teach our poets warmth and humanness—qualities in which American poets are singularly lacking—the answer must be an un-qualified yes.

XXV

Vox—et Praeterea? Maxwell Bodenheim

IT will be recalled that when the Imagists first came upon us they carried banners, and that upon one of them was inscribed their detestation of the "cosmic," and of the "cosmic" poet, who (they added) "seems to us to shirk the real difficulties of his art." No doubt if the Imagists were to issue this particular volume again they would find occasion to alter this and perhaps other statements, for here as elsewhere they sinned against one of their own cardinal doctrines—they failed to think clearly and, *ipso facto*, failed also to define with precision. Were they quite sure what they meant by the term "cosmic" poet? Did they mean, for example, Dante—or only Ella Wheeler Wilcox? The point is trifling, it may be, and yet it is not without its interest, for it indicates an error characteristic of the moment. It was not unnatural that those of our poetic

revolutionaries who, tired of the verbose senti-
mentalities and ineptitudes of the more mediocre
among their predecessors, determined to achieve
a sharper picturism in poetry, should in the first
excited survey of the situation decide that anything "cosmic," or let us say philosophic, was obviously beyond the focus of their poetic camera—
could not be "picturized." It appeared that
thought would have to be excluded—and in fact
for a year or more, under the influence of the
Imagists, the markets were flooded with a free
verse in which thought was conspicuously at a
minimum. "Pure sensation!" was the cry—a cry
which has been heard before, and will be heard
again; it arises from a question almost as old as
poetry itself—the question whether the poet
should be only a drifting sensorium, and merely
feel, or whether he should be permitted to think.
Should he be a voice, simply—or something beside? Should he occasionally, to put it collo-
quially, say something? Or should he be merely
a magic lantern, casting coloured pictures for ever
on a screen?

The question is put perhaps too starkly, and
purposely leaves out of account all of the minute
gradations by which one passes from the one ex-

treme to the other. And the occasion for the
question is Mr. Maxwell Bodenheim, who, though
already well known as a poet, has just published
his first book, "Minna and Myself." Mr. Bodenheim might well, it appears, have been one of the
Imagists. None of them, with perhaps the exception of "H. D.," can equal his delicate precision
of phrasing. None of them is more subtly pictorial. Moreover Mr. Bodenheim's theories as to
the nature of poetry (for which he has adroitly argued), such as that it should be a "coloured grace"
and that it should bear no relation to "human
beliefs and fundamental human feelings," might
seem even more clearly to define that affinity.
Yet it would be a great mistake to ticket Mr.
Bodenheim as an Imagist merely because his
poetry is sharply pictorial, or because he has de-
clared that poetry should not deal with fundamental human emotions. As a matter of fact his
theory and performance are two very different
things. One has not gone very far before detect-
ing in him a curious dualism of personality.

It is obvious, of course, that Mr. Bodenheim has
taken out of the air much that the Imagists and
other radicals have set in circulation. His poems
are in the freest of free verse: they are indeed quite

candidly without rhyme or metrical rhythm, and
resolve themselves for the most part into series of
lucid and delicate statements, of which the crisp
cadences are only perhaps the cadences of a very
sensitive prose. It is to Mr. Bodenheim's credit
that despite the heavy handicap of such a form he
makes poems. How does he do this? Not
merely by evoking sharp-edged images—if he did
only that he would be indeed simply an exponent
of "coloured grace" or Imagism—but precisely because his exquisite pictures are not merely pictures,
but symbols. And the things they symbolize are,
oddly enough, these flouted "fundamental feelings."

Mr. Bodenheim is, in short, a symbolist. His
poems are almost invariably presentations of
mood, evanescent and tenuous—tenuous, frequently, to the point of impalpability—in terms of
the visual or tactile; and if it would be an exaggeration to say that they differ from the purely
imagistic type of poetry by being, for this reason,
essentially emotional, nevertheless such a statement approximates the truth. Perhaps rather
one should say that they are the ghosts of emotions, or the perfumes of them. It is at this point
that one guesses Mr. Bodenheim's dualism. For

it seems as if the poet were at odds with the theorist: as if the poet desired to betray these "fundamental emotions" to a greater extent than the severe theorist will permit. In consequence one feels that Mr. Bodenheim has cheated not only his reader but also himself. He gives us enough to show us that he is one of the most original of contemporary poets, but one feels that out of sheer perversity he has withheld even more than he has given. There are many poets who have the *vox et praeterea nihil* of poetry, and who wisely therefore cultivate that kind of charm; but it is a tragedy when a poet such as Mr. Bodenheim, possessing other riches as well, ignores these riches in credulous obeisance to the theory that, since it is the voice, the hover, the overtone, the perfume alone which is important in poetry, therefore poetry is to be sought rather in the gossamer than in the rock. Mr. Bodenheim has taken the first step: he has found that moods can be magically described—no less than dew and roses. But poetic magic, as George Santayana has said, is chiefly a matter of perspective—it is the revelation of "sweep in the concise and depth in the clear"— and, as Santayana points out, if this is true we need not be surprised to perceive that the poet will

find greatest scope for this faculty in dealing with
ideas, particularly with philosophic ideas. . . .
And we return to our old friend the "cosmic."

Nor need Mr. Bodenheim be unduly alarmed.
For when one suggests that the contemplation of
life as a whole, or the recognition of its items as
merely minute sand-grains of that whole, or an
occasional recollection of man's twinkling unim-
portance, or a fleeting glimpse of the cruel perfection of the order of things, are among the finest
headlands from which the poet may seek an outlook, one is certainly not suggesting that poets
should be logicians. "It is not the paraphernalia
but the vision of philosophy which is sublime." If
the poet's business is vision, he can ill afford to
ignore this watch-tower. For if, like Mr. Bodenheim, he desires that poetry shall be a kind of
absolute music, "unattached with surface sentiment"—a music in which sensations are the notes,
emotions the harmonies, and ideas the counterpoint; a music of detached waver and gleam, which,
taking for granted a complete knowledge of all
things, will not be so naïve as to make statements,
or argue a point, or praise the nature of things, or
inveigh against it, but will simply employ all such
elements as the keys to certain tones—then truly

the keyboard of the poet who uses his brain as well as his sensorium will be immensely greater than that, let us say, of the ideal Imagist.

The point has been elaborated because, as has been said, it is one on which Mr. Bodenheim seems to be at odds with himself: the poems in "Minna and Myself" show him to be an adept at playing with moods, an intrepid juggler with sensations, but one who tends to repeat his tricks, and to juggle always with the same set of balls. Of the poems themselves what more needs to be said than that they are among the most delicately tinted and fantastically subtle of contemporary poems in free verse? Mr. Bodenheim's sensibility is as unique in its way as that of Wallace Stevens or of T. S. Eliot or of Alfred Kreymborg. One need not search here for the robust, nor for the seductively rhythmic, nor for the enkindling. Mr. Bodenheim's patterns are cool almost to the point of preciosity; they are, so to speak, only one degree more fused than mosaics. They must be read with sympathy or not at all. And one feels that Mr. Bodenheim is only at his beginning, and that he will eventually free himself of his conventions on the score of rhythm (with which he is experimenting tentatively) and of theme-colour. In

what direction these broadenings will lead him,
only Mr. Bodenheim can discover. One is con-
vinced, however, that he can step out with
security.

XXVI

Philosophy for the Flute:
Alfred Kreymborg

THE public, or that iridescent portion of it which occasionally thinks of such things as poetry, has not found it easy to make up its mind about Alfred Kreymborg. When his first book, "Mushrooms," appeared—a book to which he appended the disarming sub-title "A Book of Free Forms"—this iridescent fraction twinkled for a moment between indifference and derision: could a man who wrote thus be anything but charlatan? Was he serious? And the oddities of taste to which Mr. Kreymborg lent himself in the editorship of "Others" were not calculated to mitigate this impression. A good many people have from first to last thought of him as one who, with a view to obtaining any sort of publicity, has courted the bizarre in art, the aesthetically brindled, very much as a newspaper editor might court the sensational. Perhaps there is a trace of truth in this. But one must remember that Mr. Kreymborg was in the position of an editor-poet, serious in his intentions, (even if his intentions related largely—as whose do not?—to himself) but almost wholly without funds. Some sort of publicity was indispensable. And it was only too dangerously easy for one whose natural interest was in the "new" in art to heighten "newness" for this purpose to the point of novelty.

The result has been, as in most such cases, two-natured: it has made Mr. Kreymborg tolerably well-known, but on the other hand the reputation it has bestowed on him is in a sense a speckled one, the colour of which is questionable. With what, precisely of all the hues ranging from lemon-yellow through saffron to earthy brown, should one associate him? With the gelatinous erogenous quiverings of Mina Loy, the tortuously patterned logic of Marianne Moore, the syllable-eruptions with which Walter Arensberg has infected language? Or rather with the gentle skill and beauty of such poets as Wallace Stevens and Maxwell Bodenheim? Mr. Kreymborg's two small books, "Mushrooms" and "Plays for Poem-Mimes" indicate clearly enough that it is in the latter class that, now at any rate, he belongs.

But they indicate also, perhaps, that Mr. Kreymborg himself has not always from the outset been too precisely aware of this destiny.

"Mushrooms," in fact, was a book of which experiment and uncertainty were ruling motives. It was something new in poetry that Mr. Kreymborg desired, but of what nature this should be was not quite clear to him. Rhyme, one imagines him saying to himself, can, and perhaps should, be largely dispensed with; stanza-patterns certainly are not desirable where they are not inevitable; one's personality should, in the full sense of its immediate moment, be free, and colloquial; and are capital letters at the beginnings of lines any longer necessary? Into the psychological value of the latter custom one need not go; nor need one here discuss the sheer propulsive force, or value for emphasis, or for beauty of sound, of rhyme. One is more interested in Mr. Kreymborg's effort to give full rein to his personality and have it none the less, as it were, pace.

For the fact is that if we approach his work first from the technical side we find it to be something quite different from what is commonly called free verse or cadenced verse. Mr. Kreymborg is in reality a melodist, a melodist perhaps more exactly in the musical than in the metrical sense, though the result is, or should be, in the upshot, the same. The poems in Mushrooms are constantly approaching the condition of having a tune; and Mr. Kreymborg has himself told us that it is often with a definite musical tempo in mind—three-four time for example—that he writes them. It is not remarkable therefore that one feels more precision and gusto of movement in many of these poems than one does in most free verse. What is remarkable is that on the whole one feels this so seldom, relatively; or,—perhaps it would be fairer to say,—that one so seldom feels it strongly. Certain of the shorter lyrics fall clearly and deliciously enough into a piercing Mozartian pattern, a pattern which lacks perceptibly nothing through the absence of rhyme. In such cases one feels that the addition of piano accompaniment and melody for the voice would be extremely simple. This is true also of many of the brief lyric movements in the "Plays for Poem-Mimes." Observe, for example, from "Mushrooms" the opening lines of "To Circe":

Voice, voice, marvellous voice:
Come, come back to me!

[243]

SCEPTICISMS

Or, from the later volume, in "When the Willow
Nods":

> Only when the willow nods
> does the water nod:
> only when the wind nods
> does the willow nod;
> only when a cloud nods
> does the wind nod;
> and, of course, nod
> rhymes with God. . . .

In these excerpts the melody is clear enough. But
these are the exception and all too often one looks
in vain for the metrical or rhythmical clue. What
is the difficulty? Mr. Kreymborg is, as it happens, exceptionally sensitive to music, exceptionally perceptive of its values. But of this
sensitiveness and perceptiveness he carries over to
the other art, the art of word-arrangement, only
so much of music as relates to the distribution of
ictus and pause. This alone, unfortunately, will
not wholly serve. Ictus is lame, if not actually
functionless and vestigial, if it does not fall on
the right syllable, the syllable suited to the occasion by its sound; and pause, if it be distributed
without regard for the kindred pauses of idea and
orotundity, is merely unobserved. A beautiful or

rich or subtle movement in poetry derives about equally from sound-values and rhythm-values: the skilful poet knows how to synthesize them in such a way as at one moment to produce harmony, when they fall smoothly in unison, and at another to produce dissonance, when they slightly clash. Mr. Kreymborg could manage the rhythmic part of this synthesis, but his sense of sound values is deficient. He appears to be unaware of the variability of effect producible by syllabic arrangement, the felicitous alternation or repetition of deep or shallow vowels, dull or sharp consonants, or consonants richly sheathed. In this regard it is interesting to contrast him with so different a poet as Mr. John Gould Fletcher, who lacks the specifically metrical sense as conspicuously as Mr. Kreymborg possesses it, but who, on the other hand, is inferior to no poet living in his use of the colour of sound.

The result of Mr. Kreymborg's deficiency in the sense of sound-values is that his verse has about it always, whether the melodic movement is marked or slight, grave or capricious, a kind of thinness, a thinness as evident to the eye as to the ear,—evident to the eye, perhaps, as too slight a filament might be when dedicated to a task too severe, audible to the ear as the thin obstructed voice of a flute, a voice which one might conceive as being embodied, above the flute, in a waver of finest gossamer. The medium is, it is true, individual; one could not mistake a poem by Mr. Kreymborg. It has its delicate charm, whimsical or sharp; and it has also its absurdities, when the childlike candour which is the poet's favourite mood leads him to extravagances of naïve repetition. Mr. Kreymborg has, it is possible, been a little too much encouraged by admiration in this regard. His charm for us has been, always so largely a personal charm, a charm of the colloquial voice, of the intimate gesture seen through the printed page, the whimsical shy defensive twinkle or grimace, that perhaps it has become difficult for him not to overdo it. A responsive audience is demoralizing. If one can so captivate with a penny whistle's droll capricious tendernesses and innuendoes, why concern one's self with an orchestra?

Well, why indeed? . . . It is Mr. Kreymborg himself who shows us why. The fact is that he is by way of being a philosophical poet, one who is never completely happy unless he is teasing himself or his reader with the insoluble hieroglyphs of

the universe, hieroglyphs which he employs, as an
artist should, half for their own sake and half for
their value as sheer decoration.   But it is curious
to observe how step by step with Mr. Kreymborg's
development of the philosophical attitude has developed with it also one of its important germinal
components, a component which had its value and
charm during the earlier phases, but which now
threatens to become an incubus.   This component
is Mr. Kreymborg's fondness for the attitude of
childlike wonder,—for the exclamation of round-
eyed astonishment, a lyricism a trifle too consciously sheer; a note which even at the outset in
"Mushrooms," for those who do not wish in poetry
merely a saturated solution of tender personality,
manifested a disposition to become, whenever the
framework of thought was too slight, a poetic
paraphrase of the lisp and coo.   The attitude of
wonder is itself of course impeccable; one cannot
possibly quarrel with anything so profoundly and
beautifully human, or so productive, as it has
been, of the finest note in poetry.   What one re-
sents somewhat is Mr. Kreymborg's reduction of it
at times to a sort of babblement, as if he were
determined to hear the world only when it spoke
to him in monosyllables,—and not in the primal

and thundering monosyllables, the superb mono-
liths by which we measure our bewildered inse-
curity, but in those rather which suggest the
pinafore. This one forgave in the earlier volume,
for there it had about it a pleasant irresponsibility
and gusto; but in the later volume, in which Mr.
Kreymborg abandons his "free forms" for plays
in free verse, one's forgiveness is not unmixed.
For what indeed has occurred here but that Mr.
Kreymborg has made precisely a convention of this
attitude of childlike wonder, and has, in every
play here submitted, from tinkling farce to
tinkling tragedy, reduced our heaven knows not
too mature humanity to terms of mincing precocious childhood? Let us grant that once or twice
repeated this still has its exquisite charm, as of a
tiny Mozartian melody twinkling from a minute
music-box. To this charm certainly one surren-
ders in "Manikin and Minikin": in "Lima Beans"
and "Jack's House," however, one is now and then
just perceptibly annoyed by the persistent sentimentality with which the poet reduces his
personae not indeed merely to terms of childhood
but more exactly to terms of dollhood: The boy
and the girl regard each other with eyes perpetually like saucers, their mouths for ever shaped to

the "Oo"! of puppet wonder, their gestures un-
varyingly rectangular and affectedly awkward.
What, even from Mr. Kreymborg's viewpoint, is
gained by this? One perceives readily enough of
course his wish to present his *personae* "in a light,"
in the light of human futility and its charming (or
ridiculous) helplessness. The puppet, particularly in a tragic rôle, does this to perfection; it is
an artifice, or indeed a mechanism, admirably
suited to its purpose. But once done is there any
use doing it again? Is it wise of Mr. Kreymborg
to make this one note the burden of everything
he writes? The themes of "People Who Die,"
it is true, or "Blue and Green," are unalike, and
are played upon very often with great delicacy
and precision, with a subtlety of conception which
has beauty and dignity. But here also the heroes
and heroines are dolls, studiously restricting themselves to rhythms and ideas which frequently suggest nothing so much as Mother Goose. It is high
time these precocious children grew up.

And Mr. Kreymborg must surely be aware that
as long as he stages for us merely this parade of
dolls,—no matter in what lights or costumes or
charming quarrels or exquisitely naïve psychological self-searchings,—these things will be but the

surface twinkle, and the basic idea will remain "doll." The cords of a convention are about him. If Mr. Kreymborg wishes range and depth for his speculations, variety for his moods, will he not do well to abandon his whimsical flute,—not altogether, for it has its beauties of clarity and liquid modulation, its droll breakings into the squeal of falsetto,—and try now and then another instrument? There are limits after all to what one can say with a flute. And there is no doubt that Mr. Kreymborg has more to say.

XXVII

Amy Lowell as Critic

MISS LOWELL'S book, "Tendencies in Modern American Poetry," while apparently a disinterested survey of the more conspicuous strains in contemporary American poetry, is in reality no more disinterested than any other book by a partis pris critic. It is, essentially, an adroit, though in the present reviewer's opinion erroneous, piece of propaganda. Posing as an impresario, an introducer of artists, Miss Lowell is really a Svengali; she is determined to have the art of singing develop in her own way. She perceives, as other artist-critics have perceived (though she may do it unconsciously), that if her own theories of work are to be validated by an ecumenical judgment she must praise those theories when they are practised by others, judge them favourably in a manner which shall appear weightily objective, and, in every way possible, give them the focus of importance. Her right to believe these theories the best is of course incontestable. Her right to give this personal belief the air of objective analysis, or scientific judgment, is only defensible, however, if fact and reason support her. And in this respect we may question whether she has not clearly failed.

This failure rests in the framework itself of Miss Lowell's book: it is in the framework of the book that she has built up her propaganda. This propaganda is to the effect that the six poets here discussed form so many stages in an evolutionary order; and that the most highly developed of these poets, in an evolutionary sense, are the Imagists— H.D. and John Gould Fletcher. This, of course, from Miss Lowell's own viewpoint is so delightful and so nourishing a conclusion to reach that it at once becomes the critic's duty to suspect her of wish-thinking. Can she be right? Let us see, briefly, how Miss Lowell does it. In her first two poets, Robinson and Frost, Miss Lowell finds a disillusionment with the ideas of the immediate past, a desire to break away, half-inhibited, and a backward yearning toward remembered beauty in restraint (this latter Miss Lowell calls "atavism," a word which, psychologically speaking, is dead;

quite as mythological as a lamia). In the second pair of poets, Sandburg and Masters, she encounters so violent a revolt against literary and social tradition that the poets are obsessed with it and are prone to neglect beauty altogether: they destroy, but do not creatively replace. Finally in the third pair of poets, Miss Lowell finds a complete emancipation from all moral or social issues, and a complete devotion to the creation of beauty in a new way. Miss Lowell is here careful to disclaim any belief that these poets are necessarily any better than the others; they are merely, in this evolutionary sense, more advanced. . . .

Now, unfortunately, it is impossible to discuss accurately any sort of evolution except in terms of a single genus or line. It is profitless (probably) to argue whether the dog is evolutionarily in advance of the cat, the Brazilian kinkajoo in advance of the Baldwin apple, or the Jew's-harp in advance of the sonnet. These things are not related, do not evolve one from another. In much the same way, we have various different species of poet, and it is a falsification of the facts to say that one sort is necessarily in advance of another. Realists and romanticists (to use terms which are obsolescent but still meaningful) develop in parallels, not in one line: one sort of realism may be newer or more advanced than another sort of realism, but its evolution is a thing apart from the evolution of romanticism. So, too, with lyric poets, and narrative poets, and dramatic poets. They exist side by side contemporaneously, working in different directions, all of them evolving (if evolution must be insisted on), but evolving in parallel lines. One sees at once, therefore, the futility of endeavouring to relate in any evolutionary sense such a realist as Frost with such a symbolist as Fletcher. Frost, in his own genre, is quite as highly advanced as Fletcher: so is Masters, and so is Sandburg. They are working in different materials, but materials equally valid and important and true to life. Excursions in pure aesthetics will never replace psycho-realism (to coin a word), nor vice versa: the two methods are not competitive, but complementary, and capable of fusion. One may prefer romanticism in a radical style to realism in a radical style, but neither can be said, dogmatically, to be higher in the scale of evolution than the other.

In this regard, therefore, Miss Lowell's book wholly collapses. So far as truth is concerned, her evolutionary order might be inverted; if one excepts Robinson, who in point of poetic form is less radical than any of the others . . . Form! Of form, since it is absolute, the evolution can be discussed—no matter by what type of poet employed. One wonders, therefore, whether it was not the question of form which, in a vague way, Miss Lowell had in mind when she determined on an evolutionary treatment of these so dissimilar poets. Certainly, on that basis, she could have made out a better case for the order in which she had decided to arrange them.

As for the bulk of Miss Lowell's book, aside from the matter of evolution, one reads it with mixed sensations. These essays were originally lectures, and they still smack of the women's club platform. They are colloquial, occasionally careless, alternately patronizing, popular and esoteric. Coming from a poet who has to her credit so much verse of distinction it takes one a little aback to find here a prose which, as concerns style, is so undistinguished, even amateurish, and, as concerns matter, so often redundant, inaccurate, inconsistent and inept. One is grateful for what Miss Lowell gives us of the poets' biographies; one is grateful, too, for many bits of shrewd perception. The papers on H.D. and Fletcher particularly are, despite bad arrangement, interesting and now and then illuminating. But the discussions of Robinson and Frost, of Masters and Sandburg, while often eulogistic, really tell us nothing new and have that incompleteness which indicates, on the critic's part, a temperamental failure in rapprochement. Miss Lowell sees life differently from Mr. Masters (as is natural), and in consequence she cannot help thinking that Spoon River would have been truer to life if it had been a hagiology. She sees life differently from Mr. Sandburg and writes many pages in an effort to prove that millionaires are often quite human and anarchists quite vulgar. Of Mr. Frost's preoccupation with the attempt to write verse which shall have the simplicity of conversational speech and its modulations she says nothing; instead she exclaims at his failure to employ dialect in his New England poems—a failure for which we can wisely be grateful.

Taken all together, in conjunction with the fundamental falsity of her evolutionary scheme, these things compel one to conclude that a certain intellectual unripeness and sketchiness, a proneness to hasty and self-satisfying conclusions without careful or accurate survey of the facts, make of

AMY LOWELL AS CRITIC

Miss Lowell an amateur rather than a serious critic. She is engaging, clever, an industrious assimilator of current ideas, and to some degree she sifts among them the bad from the good; but the instant she enters the psychological or philosophical or reflective spheres she proves herself a child, swayed very largely by her emotions and desires. She desires to think that Aldington never wrote a metrical line, and so, without looking to see, she thinks so and says so; and she is wrong. She desires to think that the imagist method is the last word in poetry, and evolves her scheme of evolution. Miss Lowell rebukes Mr. Sandburg for admitting social propaganda into his poetry. She would do well to remember that propaganda in literary criticism is just as dangerous if the too-eager critic ignores or distorts the facts. When the scientific method is used to demonstrate anything but the truth, it invariably proves a boomerang.

XXVIII

The Ivory Tower: Louis Untermeyer as Critic

THE critic of poetry who is also a poet is apt to be the most interesting and the most unreliable of critics. He is interesting, because his contact with contemporary poetry is intimate and emotional rather than, as in the case of the somewhat hypothetical judicial critic, merely speculative and coolly selective. He is vitally concerned with the success or failure of this or that particular strain of work. This makes for warmth in his criticism, and for that sort of intensity of perception which an enthusiasm will focus on a small area. But it makes, also, for unreliability as concerns matters which lie outside of that focus. This unreliability will be diminished, of course, in the degree in which the critic is aware of his bias and makes allowance for it. Even so, it cannot be removed.

Mr. Untermeyer, who has now co-ordinated in

a book his reviews of contemporary poetry, is a pretty good specimen of this kind of critic; and it seems appropriate that his book should be examined by one of his own species, and, in particular, by one who for the most part has opposed and been opposed by Mr. Untermeyer at every turn. Mr. Untermeyer and his reviewer share, of course, certain likes and dislikes: their respective circles have, as would be inevitable, a considerable area in common. But in the main they reflect tendencies which are antagonistic, and it would perhaps be in the interests of poetic justice that these should be frankly confessed.

Mr. Untermeyer's evolution has been interesting. Leaving out of account his parodies, his first books were a volume of sentimental and traditional love poems and a volume of lyrics having the title "Challenge" and pretty well infused with the doctrine, popular a few years ago, of the "red blood" school. Both books revealed Mr. Untermeyer as essentially a conservative poet; one who did not by nature love to experiment; one who, indeed, felt no compulsion toward any kind of artistic innovation, for the patent reason that he had nothing particularly new or intransigeantly individual to say. Any traces of radicalism he possessed were either in the shape of this "red-blooded Americanism," a sort of localized "I am the master of my fate;" or in the shape of social radicalism, a desire for a more democratic, or shall I say, more socialistic, kind of democracy. The chances are that if he had been left undisturbed Mr. Untermeyer would have continued to write, proficiently and lustily enough, on these themes. . . . But Mr. Untermeyer, like many another conservative poet, was not to be left undisturbed. It was his misfortune that there were radicals maturing; and beginning about 1911 these revolutionaries began throwing their bombs into the aesthetic arena with deadly effect. The world of letters was destined for rapid changes. Masefield and Gibson first appeared, then the Georgians, then our realists Masters and Frost, then the Imagists, and Amy Lowell, and Sandburg; and finally the nomadic and unprincipled tribe of "Others."

It is to Mr. Untermeyer's credit that in this pandemonium, so distressingly not of his own choosing, he managed to keep his feet. He was sturdy and intelligent; and if he could not precisely hope to lead this somewhat capriciously enthusiastic mob, he at any rate succeeded in fol-

lowing it, with considerable discernment, and at
no great distance. . . . The successes of these
radicals, however, left him in an uncomfortable
position. Oddly enough, Mr. Untermeyer had
conceived himself to be somewhat radical—he
had, I dare say, seen himself, (which of us has
not?) as an intrepid explorer of dark continents;
and it nonplussed him a little to find his radicalism
all of a sudden so nakedly *vieux jeu*. But he
lacked neither courage nor adaptability. It was
not long before he had begun, as a poet, to bring
himself up to date, to vary the length of his lines
a bit, and, as a critic, to fight vigorously and keenly
for ideals wisely, though perhaps a little grudg-
ingly, modified. The first horrible chaos cleared
up quickly enough; and Mr. Untermeyer was soon
in possession of a consistent and well-edged policy.

This policy he now puts before us in his survey
of contemporary American poetry. It is, as we
should expect, an elaboration and broadening of
the principles underlying his own two early books;
his chief tenets are Americanism, lustihood, glorification of reality (facing of the world of fact)
democracy (a word which few of his pages lack)
and, of course, the postponed, though not to be
omitted, inevitable beauty. These tenets he

works hard, particularly those of Americanism, lustihood and democracy. These are, indeed, his touchstones. It is "Americanism" he sees, above all, in Masters, Frost, Robinson, even Amy Lowell; it is "democracy" he sees above all, in Giovannitti, Wood, Oppenheim, Sandburg, Brody, Lola Ridge; and it is chiefly for their manifestation of these qualities that, apparently, Mr. Untermeyer accords these poets the place of honour in his book, and, *ipso facto*, the place of honour in contemporary poetry. Poetry, according to Mr. Untermeyer "is expressing itself once more in the terms of democracy. This democracy is two-fold: a democracy of the spirit and a democracy of speech. This is the unifying quality that connects practically all of the poets with whom I propose to deal; it intensifies what is their inherent Americanism; and it charges their varied art with a native significance. . . ." Art, our critic goes on to say, is a community expression: away, therefore, with the pernicious doctrine of "art for art's sake"; and down with the ivory tower. Art has a human function to perform. It has no right to cloister itself, to preoccupy itself solely with beauty.

Well, these ideas are appealing, they have their

precise value. Let us grant in particular the rightness, and indeed the commonplace inevitability, of the fact that periodically a literature will renew itself by a descent into the Bethesda well of demotic speech. We may go even further, and say that from the sociological viewpoint nothing can be more interesting than the reflection of social changes and social hungers in literature. But, here, I think, we must pause. The implications become a trifle ominous. Are we to conclude from these premises that art is any the less art because it fails to satisfy a contemporary hunger for this or that social change? Are we to conclude that art is any the more richly art because it bears conspicuously and consciously the label "Made in America"? Is Poe to be judged, as an artist, inferior to Whitman because he is less nationalistic or less preoccupied with social consciousness? Or, indeed,—since Mr. Untermeyer really raises the question,—is such an art as Poe's, which as well as any illustrates the virtues and defects of the theory of art for art's sake, a whit the less a form of community expression, a whit the less satisfying to the human hunger for articulation, than such an art as Mr. Untermeyer seems to favour?

These questions, it seems to me, can intelli-

gently be answered only in the negative. It is at
this point that the line of cleavage between the
tendencies for which Mr. Untermeyer stands and
those for which his reviewer stands become most
sharply apparent. For Mr. Untermeyer's book
answers all these questions, my implication, in the
affirmative. I do not mean that he dispenses with
the aesthetic approach altogether in his appraisal
of contemporary poets: his aesthetic approach I
shall come to later. But I do mean that Mr. Untermeyer allows nationalistic and sociological con-
siderations to play an equal part with the aesthetic.
To put it curtly, he likes poetry with a message,—
poetry which is politically, from his viewpoint, on
the right side. Surely he must perceive the short-
sightedness and essential viciousness of this? Social ideas are local and temporary: they change
like the fashions, the materials with which they
deal are always in flux, and the odds are great that
what is a burning issue today will be a familiar
fact, and the occasion of a yawn, tomorrow.
These are, from the standpoint of the artist, mere
superficialities: if they are to be touched they must
be touched lightly, tangentially grazed. It is not
to the political odes of Wordsworth, Coleridge,
Swinburne, that we most joyously turn in reread-

ing those poets.   And the social problems of Shelley's "Revolt of Islam" merely excite our curiosity.

Here, then, lies the great fault of Mr. Untermeyer's book.   This bias has harmfully deflected it from the very outset, it has cast into undue prominence the work of Oppenheim, Giovannitti, Charles Erskine Scott Wood, Alter Brody; it has put a wrong emphasis on the work of Sandburg; and, *per contra*, it has thrown into a shadow by no means deserved the work of such poets as do not, in Mr. Untermeyer's opinion, fulfil their social contracts,—such poets as T. S. Eliot, John Gould Fletcher, Wallace Stevens, Maxwell Bodenheim, the Imagists, and the entire strain in poetry for which they inconspicuously stand, the strain which we indicate when we use the phrase "art for art's sake."   The work of the latter poets is not, in bulk, great: their positions are not, as concerns reputation, secure.   Yet I think there can be no question that all of them have given us poems which, judged as works of art, are clearly finer, and more universal in appeal, than anything as yet given us by Oppenheim, Giovannitti, Wood, or Brody. The latter four are, in fact—with all due allowance made for their vitality, sincerity, and frequent skill—simply, viewed as artists, mediocre.

Mere energy will not save them. It is indeed open to question whether they do not deserve the same indictment as thinkers; as deliverers of the "message." And to honour them as copiously as Mr. Untermeyer honours them is in a measure to derogate from the true value of those among whom they are placed—Frost, Masters, Amy Lowell, and Robinson.

But this sociological and nationalistic bias, while it is the prime factor in Mr. Untermeyer's error, is not the only one. It will not completely diagnose Mr. Untermeyer's case; it will not alone explain his too enthusiastic preferences, his too acrimonious antipathies. Let us revert for a moment to his love of the art that bears a message. This hunger carries with it in Mr. Untermeyer's mind homologous hungers in the spheres of metaphysics and aesthetics, hungers which reveal themselves as clearly in his poetry as in his criticism. His interests are, in short,—as was indicated earlier,—primitively naïve; he is oratorically assertive, a trifle consciously robust; and quite aside, therefore, from questions of social ethics, his predilections in poetry are for the unflinchingly masculine, the explicitly affirmative (what Nietzsche termed the "yea-saying"), the triumphantly and not too reflectively acceptant; the vigorous, in short, rather than the cerebral or oblique or disillusioned, the enthusiastic and downright or sanely sentimental rather than the interpretative or analytic or psychologically tenuous.

And here we come upon the matter of Mr. Untermeyer's aesthetic equipment, and pitch at once, flatly, upon his very serious limitations. Within these limitations Mr. Untermeyer has, if we recall his two first volumes of verse, grown remarkably; he has extended his sympathies further than one might have hoped. But, at the critical point, they fail. Beyond the delicately overtoned lyrics of de la Mare, unconventionally conventional in form, relatively simple in range, or, on the other hand, beyond the matter-of-fact incisive satires of Spoon River, or the slightly too smoothly turned etchings of Robinson, they cannot reach. And, unfortunately for Mr. Untermeyer, it is precisely in these two directions that the fruit-work is being done. In the former direction it gives us the work of H.D., of Pound (at his best), of Fletcher, of Stevens, of Bodenheim; in the latter, that of Eliot, Kreymborg, Masters, (his later vein), and, tentatively, that of various contributors to Others. What these two groups have in common is the fact that they are both after a kind of absolute poetry—a poetry which delivers no message, is imbued with no doctrine, a poetry which exists only for the sake of magic,—magic of beauty on the one hand, magic of reality on the other, but both struck at rather through a play of implication than through matter-of-fact statement. This sort of poetry is of course unmoral and unsociological. It is not idolatrous: the circumstances, the emotions, out of which it springs, are its instruments, merely, the musical strings on which it strikes, not the items in a conscious ritual. It is the be-all and end-all of such poetry that it should be a perfectly formed and felt work of art: and the greater the elaboration and subtlety consistent with such perfection the more inexhaustible will it be, the longer it will endure. Unhappily for us and for Mr. Untermeyer, this type of poetry merely excites his animosity. When it is in the Fletcher-Bodenheim-Stevens vein he grants its skilful use of word-colour, but is distressed by its apparent emptiness; when it is in the Eliot-Kreymborg-Williams vein he is annoyed by its tenuousness, baffled by its elusive use of introspection; and he takes refuge in terming it decadent, or effeminate, or morbid. It is not sufficiently affirmative for Mr.

LOUIS UNTERMEYER

Untermeyer: it does not obviously enough encourage him to believe in God, or in the divinity of man, or in the rightness of democracy, or in the beauty and immortality of life. Mr. Untermeyer suspects it of a kind of negativism. It is not frank with him, will not state its text with sufficient candour. Moreover one suspects in Mr. Untermeyer's reiterated denials of anything "new" in such work, as well as in his use of such phrases as "self-adulatory radicalism" the survival of some injury to a now hopelessly overborne belief that he is a radical himself.

It is, in other words, precisely the finer note in contemporary poetry which Mr. Untermeyer most completely misses. For two-thirds of the gamut his perceptions are, if not subtle, at any rate sound. His discussions of Frost, Robinson, Amy Lowell, Masters, are adequate, sometimes penetrating; though it would be a mistake to call them profound or to imply that Mr. Untermeyer deals more than superficially with the many aesthetic problems they raise. He says good things too, of Lindsay and Sandburg, even of Fletcher, Bodenheim and Kreymborg. But the conditions are adverse. He has not succeeded in detaching himself sufficiently from the here and now; and in consequence his examination of contemporary poetry, though ably written for the most part, is not wisely proportioned, nor intelligently discriminative, and it is subject, therefore, to rather savage revisals at the hands of time. Twenty years from now will these eulogistic chapters on Wood, Giovannitti, Wheelock, Brody, look perhaps a trifle odd by comparison with the cavalier and extremely incidental treatment accorded to such poets as Fletcher or Eliot?

If so, I think we have laid bare the reasons. Art is art,—not sociology, not philosophy. It may well use these things (and it may well be the richer for using them) but it cannot serve them. The best art is seldom doctrinaire; and when it is, the doctrine soon becomes the least vital element in it, important, perhaps, only for having supplied the initial impulse. And, moreover, art grows. It thrusts forward tentacles in new directions, develops new sensibilities. It is forever extending the sphere of man's consciousness. And it will do no good for the critic to deny this, or to call such advances meaningless.

It remains to say that in a sense Mr. Untermeyer's book is one for which we have been waiting: it is the only comprehensive survey we have had; it covers the ground thoroughly; it is always entertaining, frequently informative. The only regret of the present reviewer (who, it must be remembered, is as parti pris in one direction as Mr. Untermeyer in another) is that so able a writer should be guided by principles so specious and biasses so obvious; should so seldom get down, as it were, to aesthetic fundamentals; so seldom analyse aesthetically our successes and failures; and so largely limit himself to the pungently descriptive, to a consideration, merely, of the more superficial aspects of contemporary poetry. . . . To which of course the answer is, curtly, "de gustibus."

XXIX

Magic or Legerdemain?

IN every generation there are artists, men whose intentions are clearly enough honest, who tell us that in the act of artistic creation there is nothing mysterious or uncontrollable and that art is solely an affair of technique employed with a maximum of skill in accordance with aesthetic laws. At the beginning of a preceding chapter, that on the "Mechanism of Poetic Inspiration," I myself made statements which in this connection may, to some, appear confusing: I commented with some acerbity on the all too prevalent notion of critics and poets to the effect that there is something "mysterious" or "translunar" about poetic inspiration, something "which altogether escapes human analysis." These statements have indeed already proved misleading. I have even, as a result of them, been accused of maintaining, as Poe did, that a poem is a mathematically calculable product, a thing which can be constructed bit by bit, synthesized under the microscope in clearest view. That however is a theory which I have had no intention of maintaining. I maintain only that the *finished product* can and will profitably be submitted to analysis. The chemical contents of a substance may be fully known, and the scientist may none the less be unable to produce the same thing synthetically. A poem may be exhaustively analysed, and its constituent motives noted on a relatively fine scale, and, for that matter, it should be so analysed; but that with the knowledge thus acquired any individual could proceed to write a Kubla Khan or a Divine Comedy is—let us say—open to question.

For even if we agree in this regard with the fundamental (though not with some of the derived) principles of Freud and Kostyleff, and even though one therefore holds that the functional values of the arts in the life of man will be precisely understood, and defined (perhaps dangerously?), and the propulsive springs of the individual work of art with some clarity perceived; one does not on that account necessarily believe that the poet, who gives us a poem in which there is however small a grain of that sort of beauty which we call "magic," knows at every step in the

course of composition precisely what he is doing.
Quite, in fact, the contrary.   I do not think I have
ever believed or maintained anything but that it is
usually during a poet's best moments that his medium is least consciously under his control.   There
are, I know, poets who argue, with their own cases
in mind, that they know at every instant just what
effect they wish to obtain and how to obtain it.
One is permitted to doubt this statement, and to
discredit it is not difficult.   The most obvious
answer is simply that it is nearly always the poet
without "magic," the poet who does precisely control his medium at all moments, and who for that
reason gives us a poetry of close approximations
rather than of glittering achievement, who, naturally enough, denies the efficacy of the subconscious.
But that retort is a trifle too recriminatory and
easy.   It is more profitable to assume for the sake
of argument that such poets do, actually, strew
their verses with the jewels for which we foolishly hunger, and, having made that assumption,
to ask them whether after all they are so sure that
the strewing of them was foreseen, calculated, and
accomplished with conscious precision . . . or
whether, for that matter, they know any too well
how their jewels were originally come by.

MAGIC OR LEGERDEMAIN?

The affair is really one of misunderstanding; to throw any light upon it, however feebly, compels us to shift our ground, and to inquire a little into the state of mind of the poet during actual composition and the preliminary soundings which precede it.   There is, I suppose, no state of mind which to the poet is more exquisite, or which he would find harder to describe.   It might by some be defined as merely a heightening of ordinary consciousness: but while that is perhaps partially true, it would be more completely true to say that it is a sort of dual consciousness, heightened no doubt on its ordinary plane, but conspicuously different from the usual state of mind in that the many passages which lead downward to the subconscious are thrown open, and the communications between the two planes, upper and lower, are free and full.   The process by which this dualism is achieved may or may not be deliberate.   It may be achieved by an effort, by the premeditated touching off, as it were, of an idea which, one knows, will explode downward with ramifying fires through the mine-chambers upon which by association one desires to draw, or, quite as often, the initial explosion may be accidental, the starting of the train of fire by the merest chance of phrase encountered or itself tossed up from the subconscious in response to some pressure from the world of sense. During this state of dual consciousness there is a sense in which it is true that the poet has his subconscious under control. Even when working at most rapid intensity, he is sagacious of his quarry, and although, if at any moment interrupted with the question—"What is it that you pursue with such delight—what is it that you hope to obtain by rejecting that word and taking this, what superiority is there in this rhythm to that?" —he might be totally at a loss for his answer, none the less he feels in the most intangible of ways that he knows to the minutest detail the value of the impalpabilities with which he is at battle. He is diversely and brilliantly conscious of all this, but conscious only in a peculiar way: he is aware of more than he precisely sees. His decisions themselves are largely conscious, but the logical train by which he reaches any such decision has undergone such a synhaeresis as to have been to all intents obliterated. Regarding his decision at such-and-such a point to break, for example his regular mode of rhythm and to introduce an interlude which shall act as a voice antiphonally heard, he can hardly be said to have foreseen in advance

its effectiveness or, for that matter, even its existence.   He has, let us say, just finished the last line
of the preceding movement.   It is quite open to
him to proceed to a second movement growing logically and persuasively out of the first.   But perhaps, for some unglimpsed reason, some twinkling
signal from the depths of the subconscious which
he searches with heaven knows what intensity, he
is unsatisfied with this, he desires something else,
it is something else which is needed if his hunger is
to be appeased.   What is this?   And how shall
he find it?   Not, surely, by a reference to the
many and so ludicrously simple rules he knows,
nor even to the filed items of experience, which are
useful but incomplete: at such a moment his
salvation is only in an adamantine command to the
whole conscious realm of his mind to be silent,
and at once his entire attitude is that of one who
listens.   For his dissatisfaction with the fair
enough coin tendered him by the upper plane of
consciousness, the coin manufactured by labour and
patience and skill, is itself an indication from the
lower plane of consciousness that that consciousness has something finer to offer, something which
it will gladly surrender if only the invitation have
tact.   The sensation of dissatisfaction is, it should

be noted, not merely a negative affair. It relates
sharply to the thing with which he is dissatisfied,
hints at the specific incompleteness of that thing.
And it is about this spark-point of dissatisfaction
that he proceeds to generate, out of the fine air of
expectancy, the combustible vapour which shall
invite the explosion. It is then, if he is fortunate,
that he does not merely find, but actually hears,
the rhythm, the melody, the singular and unpre-
meditated tone of the next movement. Its superiority to what he had at first in mind is manifest. And his poem at this point takes on the
glow and impetus of which perhaps it has hitherto
not been able quite to guess the secret. It remains then only to take this tone-colour, so charmingly a gift, and give it a precision of shape—to
relate it organically, by employment of ideas akin
to those in the preceding movement, with the general theme of the poem.

If something like this, therefore, is true of the
method of poetic composition, it will be seen, when
one considers its impalpability, how wide is the
margin for error when one seeks with any exact-
ness to define it, or, with regard to its use of conscious and subconscious, to delimit it. The poet,
it is perceived, no matter how much he may call

upon the subconscious and deliver himself over to it, is at all times pretty much aware of what he is doing, and why; though of the precise reward for it he may be singularly uncertain. It is with this fact in mind that some poets belittle the value of the subconscious, underestimate, perhaps, the frequency with which they call upon it. They do not remember, when the poem is finished, at what points, or how many, they called for this assistance; nor have they the modesty to admit that those things in the poem which have greatest magic and beauty are usually not the product of skill, merely, but the skilful use of a wealth for the most part subterranean, a natural resource, a wealth to which they have been given access occasionally, but a wealth in the deposit of which they have played as little conscious part as the surface of the earth plays in the crystallization of diamonds. One cannot be a poet without a fine sensibility; one's sensibility is hardly controllable; and the greater part of its deposit has been accumulated long before the poet is aware of its existence.

This is not to say that anybody can be a great poet by making drafts on his subconscious. One cannot dig up jewels from a commonplace sensi-

bility, though quartz crystals may be plentiful.
But in the case of the poet who is, however intermittently, a genuine poet, one may safely say, I
think, that it is when he is most the craftsman
that he is least magically the poet. Craftsmanship is the skill with which the poet turns his subconscious treasure to account. Without that application, no matter how deft it may be, mere skill,
operating, as it were, in the air, will only approximate and imitate and endeavour to deceive. It is
a thing done with hands, a legerdemain, not magic;
one soon perceives the trick, and if one enjoys it
one does so with the intellectual coolness of admiration, not with full emotional surrender, the
uncontrolled surrender of one's own aroused subconscious. . . . When craftsmanship induces that
surrender it proves itself to be more than craftsmanship. It discloses its essentially compulsory
nature. And that the compulsions which give it
colour are often analysable is not to say that the
magic it achieves is a magic which the poet can
altogether calculate.

XXX

Appendix: A Note on Values

I

IN the course of rereading the preceding papers for the last time before sending them off to the printer, I find many things which, as no doubt even my most sympathetic reader will agree, ought to disquiet me. I have confessed with some candour in the introduction that perhaps the ruling motive of my activities as a critic has been a desire, partly conscious and partly unconscious, to secure an understanding and recognition of the particular sorts of poetry which I discover myself, in this singular world, doomed to write; but I begin to wonder, at this point, how honest or how complete that confession can be considered to be. In what way,—when I write a critique, largely laudatory of John Gould Fletcher, or of Maxwell Bodenheim, or of Jean de Bosschère,—do I clearly advance any interest of my own? That I do so at all in these and in other instances is, I think, open to question. If the methods of such poets as these are exclusively right, and if these are the methods upon which posterity will set for ever the seal of durability, it is obvious enough that myself the critic has dealt myself the poet a shrewd blow in the back. In my attempt to be honest with my reader have I been a trifle dishonest with myself? It is not too precisely demonstrable that the virtues for which I praise Fletcher or Bodenheim, or Masters or Hueffer, or Lawrence or Eliot, are the virtues at which, in the course of a struggling evolution, my own poetry might be said to aim. They are, in fact, often essentially different. An error has here been detected: in my introduction I ignored the fact that an artist may, and often does, react sympathetically to a species of art quite antipathetic to his own. In this error I may possibly, therefore, have misled my reader: he may have concluded, reading the book in this light, that the notes of Fletcher or of Bodenheim or of Masters or of de Bosschère or of Amy Lowell or of Eliot or of Gibson or of Abercrombie, since I gave them about equal consideration, are regarded by me as notes discoverably on a parity of importance in my own work. Well, I have been accused of chameleonism, and to some degree of it I have pleaded guilty; but to assume such a gift of histrionism as this would be fantastic. Let it be considered sufficient if I say that in this regard the range of my tastes is wider than that of my abilities. When I praise Eliot or Frost or Bodenheim or William Carlos Williams, let some slight trace of disinterestedness be conceded to me. Or is it—on the other hand—merely cowardice?

II

But to be exact, the whole question at issue is far too complex for so curt an answer, whether negative or affirmative. It is true that a poet-critic will tend to praise, in the work of his contemporary poets, that sort of work most sympathetic with his own; but human temperaments are amazingly unlike, and the chances are much against his ever finding a poet with a temperament which resembles his own in more than one tiny particular. Here, indeed, we touch another spring of widespread, though unconscious, dishonesty in all criticism. For it is precisely by these tiny particulars, often of so slight artistic importance, that the course of the artist-critic is most deflected. I have just remarked that Fletcher's

work was remarkably unlike my own,—crediting
myself therefore with some nobility for praising
it; but it would be more completely true to add
that nevertheless when I read the work of Fletcher
I detect in it, no matter how much his technique
may at moments alienate or alarm me, some subtle
indefinable scarcely apprehensible kinship with
my own; and this kinship outweighs all other con-
siderations. Not the least of the critic's embar-
rassments is the fact that these subtle kinships are
totally untranslatable: they are so impalpable, they
are so purely, often, in the realm of sensation, they
resist so mercurially any effort to pin them to the
walls of thought, that in most cases, since he is
moved to praise, the critic will find himself praising his poet for reasons quite other than those
which originally moved him. Reduced to a single sentence perhaps his genuine reaction to such a
poet would be "Well! this poet feels the same way
about that word that I do"; or "his sense of
rhythm is curiously like mine, with certain slight
and intriguing differences"; or "it is quite clear
that he found that out for himself—just as I did."
And such a reaction is not, as it may at first appear,
an exceptional sort of vanity. All human judgments or tastes reduce themselves under pressure

to the terms of the pathetic ego which stands as judge. It is hypocrisy to pretend anything else. But it is unfortunate, just the same, that critics so seldom lay bare these tiny but determinant factors of like or dislike, and so frequently allow them to colour their attitude toward other parts of an artist's work with which these factors have little or nothing to do. Because Matthew Arnold was a teacher, or a Victorian, or wrote occasionally, as it were, from Rugby Chapel, is no adequate reason for refusing to like "Dover Beach" or his translation of Maurice de Guérin's "Centaur."

III

But my kindly imaginary interlocutor asks me, at this point, how it is, if we like a work of art only because it reflects ourselves, or because it gives expression to some part of us which was inarticulate, or consciousness to some part of us which was unconscious, that it is possible for us to like so many and so dissimilar kinds of work. The answer is simple. It is precisely because, on the whole, the reflections of the human organism, or consciousness, in the work of any particular artist, are so tiny and so incomplete, that we are compelled, if we are to discover ourselves with anything like completeness or find ourselves mirrored at full length, to gather our reflections in splintered fragments, to assemble the portrait bit by bit. If the poet-critic, therefore, sets about composing a self-portrait which shall never employ a stroke in the first person singular, but employ only those aspects of himself which he finds in his contemporaries—an undertaking which may or may not be conscious, usually not—it should be perceived at once that the process will be laborious and confused, that it will lead him at many points far afield, and that if the resultant portrait is to attain anything like completeness it will necessarily be forced to draw, for some items, on sources which at first glimpse might appear unpromising. Confused it must, certainly, seem to the reader, provided that the reader has at all been let into the secret; provided that the poet-critic has at all confessed what he himself may not have realized, the essential self-portrayal of any kind of criticism. For what will be the key to this parade of likes and dislikes—at what points is one to presume there was an intention of emphasis? It would be simple enough, no doubt, if any human organism maintained a standard rate of efficiency, burned at a standard degree of intensity, never varying in luminosity or height. But the human organism is variable. Its identity is lost if a section of it be frozen for analysis; its identity is largely in its motion; and a motion so irregular is incommensurable and unpredictable. The poet-critic is a creature of varying moods. He dislikes today what he will like tomorrow. He finds his tastes changing, fed to satiety, outgrown, returned to in a modified form. Moreover his perceptions cannot be standardized: they are clearer at one time than at another, and he is not likely to perceive this variability. At what degree of clarity shall one say that his perceptions are most in character—when he says he likes So-and-so, for such-and-such reasons, or when he likes somebody else for reasons obviously contradictory? To this question there can be no downright answer. One can surmise, taking into account all the evidence, but one can do no more—unless the critic himself comes forward, key in hand.

IV

At this point it would be appropriate for me to supply a kind of glossary of the foregoing pages, explaining in the case of each study how I had happened to take toward the particular poet the particular attitude disclosed. Mr. Bodenheim, for instance, has said to me, shrewdly enough, that my estimate of his work is less than just because I go out of my way, apparently, to condemn it for its lack of philosophical background. "Why," remarks Mr. Bodenheim—"drag in philosophy (which I assure you does not concern me)—except to advertise a quality in poetry at which your own work is aimed?" Well, there we are. I like poetry which plays with ideas quite as joyously as with moods or sensations. I should regret it extremely if during any considerable part of my life—(for at all events it could hardly last longer) mood-symbolism and impressionism of this kind, exquisite and fragmentary, should attain such a popularity as to exclude from the public attention any work which differed from it. It is of course ridiculous, as Mr. Bodenheim might observe, to insist that a mosaic should have for its background a temple or cathedral; but it seems to me not amiss, at a moment when filigree exacts so much attention, to remind those who peer in dark corners of wall or floor for delicate bits of tracery that above their heads are ceiling and sky. Architecture, whether human or superhuman, is being too often overlooked.

APPENDIX

V

To pursue this method any further into the realm of autobiography, however, would be too painfully minute and dull. It would, indeed, necessitate a second book longer than the first, a book of which the nature would be psychological rather than literary. A considerable portion of it would have to deal with my personal acquaintance with my fellow poets, and with the effect this has had upon my essays in criticism. Is one necessarily kinder to a poet whom one has encountered in the flesh, particularly if one has found him agreeable? No,—one is merely more urbane. One spares him certain sharpnesses, no doubt, the more brutal of one's weapons are abstained from, one may even make a more determined effort than otherwise to find out his good qualities, but essentially one's attitude is unshaken. . . . That is, if one is honest. But I confess that in this regard as in others I am only human. There are one or two instances in which personal acquaintance seems to have given me an insight into a poet's work which not even the resultantly increased attention could otherwise have done. Perhaps one loses a trace of one's neutrality. It is possible

[289]

that one should refrain from acquaintanceship altogether, and make of one's self a machine for recording sensations, as exact, within its advertised limits, as is psychologically attainable. It would be one's reward, of course, to be considered egotistical and dishonest.

VI

I refrain from further autobiography, therefore; but there remains one point which in the interests of justice should be illuminated. It is impossible to supply for every critical study the complete personal key, but there is a pass-key to the present collection which should not be overlooked. It will be observed that throughout this book I have seldom made, as regards any specific poet, flat assertions of importance, or rank: what values I have employed are for the most part comparative, or implied merely in the length and seriousness of the treatment. If I were asked, for example, whether I considered any of the poets with whom I deal great poets, or poets nearly great, or poets who had attained to a power or perfection, at moments, which was likely to preserve their names for an indefinite period, I should preserve an embarrassed silence. I do not know. As concerns

the greater number of them the answer would be
unqualifiedly negative. If I have treated them
seriously, particularly those poets who are American, it is largely because they have a certain position, because they have raised issues which cannot
be flippantly dismissed, must be squarely met.
For the present, the majority of our poets are not
so much poets as symptoms. And, for that matter, at a moment such as this, which seems so
clearly a prelude rather than a performance, it is
the symptoms which are most important. No further apology seems necessary.

VII

The point is one on which I should like to di-
gress, if indeed digression is theoretically possible
in such notes as these, of which digression is the
principle. I am asked whether I do not consider
that certain of the works of Robert Frost, or Edgar
Lee Masters, or Amy Lowell, or Vachel Lindsay,
have the qualities of the finest art. And here I
must confess that I am much harder to please than
even the studies which compose this book would
suggest. Because I enjoy the work of Masters,
or Lindsay or Miss Lowell is no reason,—as too
many American critics seem to think it is,—for

supposing the work "great" or "fine," or whatever word one wishes to use for defining that supremest of pleasures one derives from a work of art. The pleasures, of this sort, which contemporary poetry affords me are for the most part on a quite secondary plane: the moments at which they rise to the other plane are few. To this secondary plane I should unhesitatingly relegate such favourites, delightful as they are, as "The Congo" or "Patterns"—no, not unhesitatingly, but I should do it. We are brilliant, we are clever to the point of brilliance, in such poems, but we are not fine. Where indeed in the work of any contemporary American poet shall we discover a consistent unison of power and fineness? We have, I think, no such poet. The great poet is not, conspicuously at any rate, amongst us. We have isolated poems which achieve the unison just mentioned—we have Robinson's "Ben Jonson Entertains a Man from Stratford," we have Eliot's "Love Song of J. Alfred Prufrock," we have the Blue and Green and White Symphonies of Fletcher, two or three pseudo-translations from the Chinese by Pound, "Home Burial" by Frost, and perhaps a dozen or two shorter things of exquisite beauty,—such as "Peter Quince at the

Clavier" by Stevens. And then there is "Spoon
River."

VIII

It is, I know, unpopular at present, to employ
in criticism what is known as the comparative
method. A work of art should be estimated in accordance as it achieves what it purports to achieve,
not in accordance as it achieves something else.
One should not expect an intaglio to shelter us
from a winter wind. But that theory has its limits: shall the rotten apple be excused for its rottenness, on the ground that the rottenness is perfect?
Or has one a right to compare it with something a
little more attractive and sustaining? I like, for
example, some of the racy titbits offered in the
two "Others" anthologies; I like, equally within
their limits, "Patterns" or "The Congo"; but have
I not the right to see, beyond and above these,
and overshadowing them, "Modern Love" by
George Meredith, or "Emblems of Love" by Lascelles Abercrombie or "An Anthem of Earth" by
Francis Thompson? Set "Patterns" against a
part of "Modern Love" or "The Congo" against
"An Anthem of Earth"; they will not lose their
charm of colour, their superficial brightness, but

observe how immediately they appear loose and amateurish; their essential second-rateness is exposed. That I feel it in this way is not, I think, mere idiosyncrasy. It is not that I do not like the stuff of which "Patterns" or "The Congo" is made: that objection would be idiosyncratic; it is because I am not satisfied with the manner in which they are made, with the skill of the artist, it is because they seem to me incomplete and shoddy as works of art, intermittently felt and intermittently performed, neither finely perceived nor finely executed, that, for all the pleasure they give me, I must withhold from them a higher estimate. They are the performance, insecure and imprecise, of amateurs remarkably gifted, not the performance of artists for whom precision and beauty of finish are inevitable. The trouble is at bottom, no doubt, that the sensibility of the poet is not, in either case, sufficiently rich or varied or subtle, extends too little, in the one case, beyond brilliant superficialities of colour and external shape, too little in the other case beyond the powerful commonplaces of gusto and rhythm and rhetoric. The finer aspects of sense, the finer shades of emotion, and those crepuscular realms which lie

between sensation and thought, but to which the
approach is tactile, have to both poets been denied.
The misfortune is a common one in the history of
poetry: let us remember such poets as Campbell
and Edwin Arnold; when we are tempted to rate
Lindsay too high on the ground that he is from
the American point of view so charmingly autoch-
thonous, let us recall the "Ingoldsby Legends."

IX

I have emphasized these two instances chiefly
because they are so typical.   Their artistic incompleteness is characteristic of contemporary American poetry, and I should like it to be understood
that it is only with this basic reservation in mind
that the relatively serious discussions which compose this book should be received.   It is not a
question of radical as against reactionary: it is not
a question of American as against European: it is
simply and solely a question of whether the given
poem has beauty, subtlety, intensity, and depth,
or whether it has not, and in what degree.   That
it is in free verse or a sonnet, that it deals with
the purely local and indigenous or not, is not necessarily of great consequence.   All that is necessary

SCEPTICISMS

is that it should be the work of an artist, achieved in a moment of maximum efficiency: a sort of efficiency which we may leave the psychologist to explain.

SELECTIVE BIBLIOGRAPHY

Abercrombie, Lascelles: Interludes and Poems. John Lane Co.

Emblems of Love. John Lane Co.

Aldington, Richard: Images. The Four Seas Co.

Bodenheim, Maxwell: Minna and Myself. Pagan.

Bosschère, Jean de: The Closed Door. John Lane Co.

Bradley, William Aspenwall: Old Christmas. Houghton, Mifflin Co.

Branch, Anna Hempstead: The Shoes that Danced. Houghton, Mifflin Co.

Rose of the Wind. Houghton, Mifflin Co.

Brooke, Rupert: Collected Poems. John Lane Co.

Bynner, Witter: Grenstone Poems. Frederick A. Stokes Co.

Davies, W. H.: Collected Poems. Alfred A. Knopf.

H. D.: Sea Garden. Houghton, Mifflin Co.

De la Mare, Walter: The Listeners. Henry Holt & Co.

Peacock Pie. Henry Holt & Co.

Eliot, T. S.: Prufrock and Other Observations. Alfred A. Knopf.

Poems. Richmond Hogarth Press.

Evans, Donald: Two Deaths in the Bronx. Nicholas L. Brown.

SCEPTICISMS

Fletcher, John Gould: Irradiations: Sand and Spray.
Houghton, Mifflin Co.

Goblins and Pagodas. Houghton, Mifflin Co.

Japanese Prints. The Four Seas Co.

The Tree of Life. The Macmillan Co.

Frost, Robert: A Boy's Will. Henry Holt & Co.

North of Boston. Henry Holt & Co.

Mountain Interval. Henry Holt & Co.

Gibson, Wilfrid Wilson: Collected Poems. The Macmillan Co.

Giovannitti, Arturo: Arrows in the Gale. Hillacre
Bookhouse.

Graves, Robert: Fairies and Fusiliers. Alfred A.
Knopf.

Hardy, Thomas: The Dynasts. The Macmillan Co.

Poems of the Past and Present. The Macmillan Co.

Satires of Circumstance. The Macmillan Co.

Time's Laughing Stocks. The Macmillan Co.

Hodgson, Ralph: Poems. The Macmillan Co.

Hueffer, Ford Madox: On Heaven and Other Poems.
John Lane Co.

Collected Poems. Max Goschen.

Some Imagist Poets. (First, second and third series.)
Houghton, Mifflin Co.

Johns, Orrick: Asphalt and Other Poems. Alfred A.
Knopf.

Kreymborg, Alfred: Mushrooms. Alfred A. Knopf.

Plays for Poem-Mimes. Others.

Kreymborg, Alfred (editor): Others (first and second
series). Alfred A. Knopf.

SELECTIVE BIBLIOGRAPHY

Lawrence, D. H.: Poems. B. W. Huebsch.

Look! We Have Come Through. B. W. Huebsch.

Lindsay, Vachel: General William Booth Enters Into Heaven and Other Poems. The Macmillan Co.

The Congo and Other Poems. The Macmillan Co.

The Chinese Nightingale. The Macmillan Co.

Lowell, Amy: Sword Blades and Poppy Seed. The Macmillan Co.

Men, Women, and Ghosts. The Macmillan Co.

Can Grande's Castle. The Macmillan Co.

Six French Poets. The Macmillan Co.

Tendencies in Modern American Poetry. The Macmillan Co.

Lowes, John Livingston: Convention and Revolt in Poetry. Houghton, Mifflin Co.

Masters, Edgar Lee: Spoon River Anthology. The Macmillan Co.

The Great Valley. The Macmillan Co.

Toward the Gulf. The Macmillan Co.

Masefield, John: Poems. The Macmillan Co.

Plays. The Macmillan Co.

Matthews, E. Powys: Coloured Stars. Fifty Asiatic Love Poems. Houghton, Mifflin Co.

Monro, Harold: Trees. Poetry Bookshop.

Strange Meetings. Poetry Bookshop.

Monroe, Harriet (editor): The New Poetry, An Anthology. The Macmillan Co.

Nichols, Robert: Ardours and Endurances. Frederick A. Stokes Co.

SCEPTICISMS

Pound, Ezra: Lustra. Alfred A. Knopf.

Pavannes and Divisions. Alfred A. Knopf.

(editor): Des Imagistes. An Anthology. Boni & Liveright.

Ridge, Lola: The Ghetto. B. W. Huebsch.

Robinson, Edwin Arlington: Captain Craig. The Macmillan Co.

Children of the Night. Charles Scribner's Sons.

The Town Down the River. Charles Scribner's Sons.

The Man Against the Sky. The Macmillan Co.

Merlin. The Macmillan Co.

Sandburg, Carl: Chicago Poems. Henry Holt & Co.

Cornhuskers. Henry Holt & Co.

Squire, J. C.: Poems. Alfred A. Knopf.

Stevens, Wallace: See The New Poetry. 1st and 2nd Others Anthologies.

Tietjens, Eunice: Profiles from China. Alfred A. Knopf.

Untermeyer, Louis: The New Era in American Poetry. Henry Holt & Co.

Williams, William Carlos: Al Que Quiere. The Four Seas Co.

Waley, Arthur (translator): 170 Chinese Poems. Alfred A. Knopf.

INDEX

INDEX

INDEX

INDEX

INDEX

Date Due